Cambridge Elements ≡

Elements in Current Archaeological Tools and Techniques
edited by
Hans Barnard
Cotsen Institute of Archaeology
Willeke Wendrich
Politecnico di Torino

CULTURAL BURNING

Bruno David
Monash University

Michael-Shawn Fletcher
The University of Melbourne

Simon Connor
Australian National University

Virginia Ruth Pullin
The University of Melbourne

Jessie Birkett-Rees
Monash University

Jean-Jacques Delannoy
Université Savoie Mont Blanc

Michela Mariani
University of Nottingham

Anthony Romano
The University of Melbourne

S. Yoshi Maezumi
Max Planck Institute for Geoanthropology

COTSEN INSTITUTE OF
ARCHAEOLOGY AT UCLA

T0311465

CAMBRIDGE
UNIVERSITY PRESS

CAMBRIDGE
UNIVERSITY PRESS

Shaftesbury Road, Cambridge CB2 8EA, United Kingdom

One Liberty Plaza, 20th Floor, New York, NY 10006, USA

477 Williamstown Road, Port Melbourne, VIC 3207, Australia

314–321, 3rd Floor, Plot 3, Splendor Forum, Jasola District Centre, New Delhi – 110025, India

103 Penang Road, #05–06/07, Visioncrest Commercial, Singapore 238467

Cambridge University Press is part of Cambridge University Press & Assessment, a department of the University of Cambridge.

We share the University's mission to contribute to society through the pursuit of education, learning and research at the highest international levels of excellence.

www.cambridge.org
Information on this title: www.cambridge.org/9781009485302

DOI: 10.1017/9781009485340

First published 2024

A catalogue record for this publication is available from the British Library

ISBN 978-1-009-48530-2 Hardback
ISBN 978-1-009-48529-6 Paperback
ISSN 2632-7031 (online)
ISSN 2632-7023 (print)

Cambridge University Press & Assessment has no responsibility for the persistence or accuracy of URLs for external or third-party internet websites referred to in this publication and does not guarantee that any content on such websites is, or will remain, accurate or appropriate.

Cultural Burning

Elements in Current Archaeological Tools and Techniques

DOI: 10.1017/9781009485340
First published online: May 2024

Bruno David
Monash University

Michael-Shawn Fletcher
The University of Melbourne

Simon Connor
Australian National University

Virginia Ruth Pullin
The University of Melbourne

Jessie Birkett-Rees
Monash University

Jean-Jacques Delannoy
Université Savoie Mont Blanc

Michela Mariani
University of Nottingham

Anthony Romano
The University of Melbourne

S. Yoshi Maezumi
Max Planck Institute for Geoanthropology

Author for correspondence: Bruno David, bruno.david@monash.edu

Abstract: This Element addresses a burning question – how can archaeologists best identify and interpret cultural burning, the controlled use of fire by people to shape and curate their physical and social landscapes? This Element describes what cultural burning is and presents current methods by which it can be identified in historical and archaeological records, applying internationally relevant methods to Australian landscapes. It clarifies how the transdisciplinary study of cultural burning by Quaternary scientists, historians, archaeologists and Indigenous community members is informing interpretations of cultural practices, ecological change, land use and the making of place. This title is also available as Open Access on Cambridge Core.

Keywords: cultural burning, firestick farming, landscape archaeology, landscape management, environmental history

ISBNs: 9781009485302 (HB), 9781009485296 (PB), 9781009485340 (OC)
ISSNs: 2632-7031 (online), 2632-7023 (print)

Contents

1 Introduction

Archaeologists are good at reading the past through artefacts and the sites that contain them. Those artefacts and sites are often positioned in broader geographies, such as through distribution maps that show how cultural practices spread across the landscape through time, and how the human occupation of places articulated with habitat characteristics. The relationships that people established with the landscape generated environmental and ecological change, such as through forest clearance for gardening or agriculture. One such theme that has remained a blindspot in much of the world is how people in the past used fire to manage their landscapes. The ability to make and use fire has long been a central theme in human evolution, but the focus has been on the origins of fire as a tool to create heat and for cooking, and more rarely to treat rock to enhance its flaking qualities when making stone tools. Yet people have long used fire in other ways too, in particular to transform and manage entire habitats into more liveable environments. 'Cultural fire' or 'cultural burning' is how such landscape-scale burning practices are often referred to. While the deep-time history of cultural burning has largely been ignored by archaeologists and palaeoecologists in many parts of the world – probably because such fires do not result in the production of 'artefacts' as conventionally defined, and therefore may at first glance seem intractable archaeologically – in recent years, it has begun to call for attention. There are two reasons for this. First, there has been slowly increasing recognition that Indigenous peoples in various parts of the world have long used cultural burning to manage their environments. As a cultural practice, archaeologists are therefore interested, given that archaeology is concerned with understanding the cultural past. Second, catastrophic wildfires, often caused by climate change, have increasingly impacted many parts of the world in recent years. Their heavy toll on human life, health, ecosystems, resources and economies has prompted intense scrutiny of fire management as it is currently practised. In the search for sustainable alternatives, a growing interest in Indigenous cultural burning has emerged.

The result is now an increasing general interest in better understanding the deep-time history of Indigenous cultures by researching patterns and trends in landscape engagements. Cultural burning is a global cultural practice (Huffman 2013; Snitker et al. 2022), developed and promoted for a variety of different reasons that are closely related to local cultural protocols, environmental conditions and events. Essentially, different cultural groups have their own ways and reasons for doing cultural burning. Academic researchers are investigating these ways and reasons around the world, often together in partnership with Indigenous communities, such as in the Amazon rainforest (Maezumi et al. 2022), eastern South Africa (Huffman 2009) and North America (Adlam et al. 2022; Hoffman et al. 2022; Larson et al. 2020; Long et al. 2021; Whitehair et al. 2018). This Element presents case studies from Australia, where cultural burning has a particularly deep temporal reach, and investigates Quaternary science methods for tracing cultural burning practices in Australia and around the world. These new studies and ancestral practices on the use of fire to prepare and manage broad landscapes has been called 'caring for Country' by many Australian Aboriginal and Torres Strait Islander peoples, and feature prominently in 'Whole-of-Country' plans aimed at managing landscapes for current and future generations. In Australia, research into the deep-time history of cultural burning, the learning about its practices from Aboriginal Traditional Owners and its application to the landscape as a wildfire management tool are growing.

Yet the question remains: where, and when, did people use fire as a strategy to manage their environments? And how can such research even be attempted in Quaternary science, given that wildfires also heat sediments, produce charcoal and affect vegetation communities? Are there Quaternary science methods by which collaborating researchers can investigate cultural approaches to managing the landscape deep into the past? This is the topic of this Element.

1.1 Indigenous Knowledge and Managed Landscapes

In some parts of the world, Indigenous communities have vast reserves of cultural burning knowledge and expertise handed down from generation to generation. Such knowledge is often unparalleled in its depth, lived experience and interconnectedness. In some regions of Australia where Indigenous rights to traditional lands are recognised through legislation, Indigenous communities continue to burn Country as a way to manage vegetation, fauna and social relationships (see Section 2 for examples of how this is done). In recent decades, government authorities responsible for managing the environment – such as National Parks, fire authorities and government departments coordinating various kinds of climate-change and environmental sustainability programmes – have tried to emulate aspects of Indigenous cultural burning, with mixed success. These largely non-Indigenous forms of cultural burning are typically referred to as 'prescribed burning'; we distinguish in this Element Indigenous 'cultural burning' strategies from institutional 'prescribed burning' programmes, both of which can also be distinguished from uncontrolled 'wildfires' (called 'bushfires' in Australia). All three types of fires concern landscape-scale fires.

As a basis for decision-making and policy change, governments and management authorities often request quantitative data by which to illustrate fire trends, such as those captured on graphs and timelines, easily communicable to landscape management authorities and the public alike. Long-term cultural burning records have been virtually non-existent among societies without writing, because it is only recently that researchers have developed methods by which to distinguish evidence of cultural burning (and prescribed burning) from wildfires in sedimentary records. Yet where living Indigenous knowledge on fire management is rich, there is the problem that colonial structures embedded in today's governments render them virtually blind to Indigenous knowledge. This is because Indigenous knowledge tends to be more holistic, embodied and place-based, whereas a predominant colonial viewpoint is predicated on short-term results, disembodiment from broader practices and placelessness in an attempt to find 'universal truths' in a 'nature' that is often imagined as separate from people and culture. However, when conducted appropriately and in partnership with Indigenous communities, scientific research can act to bridge this conceptual divide. There is emerging interest among researchers in both putting additional scientific weight behind Indigenous knowledge and adding new kinds of knowledge such as patterns and trends from the Quaternary sciences (Fletcher et al. 2021a). Needless to say, but best said for the sake of clarity, by 'researchers' we here mean all knowledge-holders in the research, including academic and community participants, Indigenous and non-Indigenous. These perspectives can help influence policy decisions in areas where First Nations peoples have played a major role in creating the landscape, and may provide more appropriate ways of living in changing environments.

Quaternary science methods have the capacity to reveal details about wildfires and cultural burning in the past. These include information on where, when, how much and how often fire was a feature of past landscapes. Analyses can reveal what was burned and the temperatures at which it burned. They can reconstruct past vegetation and biodiversity patterns in relation to fire. However, it is important to keep in mind that these methods are still under development and in themselves have limited capacity to look past the research materials and quantitative data. As discussed in this Element, cultural burning goes far beyond the realm of scientific quantification and pervades cultural, social, economic, environmental and spiritual dimensions of Indigenous peoples' existence and sense of place.

Here we detail a number of approaches and methods palaeoecologists, archaeologists, Indigenous communities and historians have adopted to examine past landscape-scale fire regimes, especially as they relate to past cultural burning. We begin Section 2 by reviewing key principles of cultural burning from the literature through two different case studies from different parts of

Australia. This is followed in Section 3 by a demonstration of how art history can reveal significant details of past cultural burning dating back to the early years of colonialism. In Section 4, we then introduce Quaternary science methods by which to research deep-time histories of cultural burning. Section 5 then explores an archaeological and palaeoecological case study. We then conclude with a number of potential avenues for future research into cultural burning in collaboration with Indigenous communities and landowners.

2 What is Cultural Burning? Caring for Country with Fire

In 1969, archaeologist Rhys Jones introduced the concept of 'fire-stick farming' to the literature. Jones was referring to the widespread Australian Aboriginal practice of 'burning Country', whereby tracts of land are 'cleaned' by putting them to the torch, lightly burning the undergrowth of vegetation and transforming the land into managed estates. Jones (1969: 225) noted that eighteenth- and nineteenth-century European explorers to Australia, 'seeing Australia from the sea, reported that the coastlines were dotted with fires. Peron, in 1802, sailing up the Derwent [River] in southeast Tasmania, said that "wherever we turned our eyes, we beheld the forests on fire."' He continued:

> In Tasmania it was customary for the Aborigines to carry their smouldering fire-sticks with them, and they set fire to the bush as they walked along. G. A. Robinson, who lived with them for the best part of 5 years, has hundreds of descriptions of their setting fire to the bush, of distant Aboriginal fires, and of large areas of countryside freshly burnt by them. (Jones 1969: 225)

Those fires lit by Aboriginal families right across Australia, Jones emphasised, were burned for a range of reasons, many or all often acting together: (1) to *signal* to kin and other community members where they were, and that they were indeed in parts of the landscape they were entitled to be in; (2) to *clear the ground* of thick undergrowth, especially to rid travelling routes and camping grounds of snakes that may hide in leaf litter and thick grass; (3) to *hunt and forage* for small fauna, to make their tracks on sandy ground easier to see and follow, to clear vegetation that masked animal burrows, and to burn or flush fauna from vegetation cover; (4) to *regenerate plant foods* by burning old grass and scrub, fertilise the ground with ash and release seeds from their capsules among a broad range of fire-adapted vegetation types; (5) for *fun*; (6) to *modify and maintain vegetation communities* to create more open, park-like landscapes for human habitation, such as mosaics of grassland and open woodland (Jones 1969). Many Aboriginal peoples and Torres Strait Islanders have spoken and written about such cultural burning (e.g. see the voices in Bright & Marranunggu 1995; Green 1995; Garde et al. 2009; Federation of Victorian Traditional Owner

Corporations, no date; Yunupingu 1995). In 2011, Bill Gammage expanded greatly on the archival evidence for Aboriginal fire-stick farming across the continent in his book *The Biggest Estate on Earth: How Aborigines Made Australia* (see also Section 3).

Much of Jones's notion of 'fire-stick farming' focused on the way that controlled fires worked to modify and manage vegetation communities to increase plant and animal productivity, thereby acting as a landscape-scale technology integral to the subsistence economy. But Jones also recognised the embeddedness of cultural fires in social, territorial and cosmological life and everyday experience. Today the label 'fire-stick farming' is still commonly used, but it is more often referred to by a range of other terms that better reflect its social and cultural dimensions: mosaic burning, Aboriginal burning, controlled fires, cultural burning, anthropic burning, 'burn grass' and so forth (see e.g. Bright & Marranunggu 1995; Federation of Victorian Traditional Owner Corporations, no date; Rose 1995). It has been a way of looking after Country practiced by Aboriginal and Torres Strait Islander communities across most, if not all, of Australia until the early colonial period, and that environmentally and ecologically shaped the Australian continent. While in some parts of Australia burning practices ceased or were interrupted in the face of nineteenth- and twentieth-century colonial appropriations of land and related social pressures and disruptions, cultural burning is making a return across many parts of the nation, especially in those regions where Aboriginal families have returned to customary lands. In other parts of Australia, it never ceased (e.g. Bright & Marranunggu 1995; Yunupingu 1995). It is also increasingly used as a strategy to inhibit devastating wildfires in recently un-managed forests. Fire management authorities and land-care groups across the nation are now learning from and engaging Aboriginal knowledge-holders to apply or adapt forms of cultural burning to the environment (e.g. Higgins 2020). 'Prescribed burning', also called 'hazard reduction burning' (Binskin et al. 2020: 6) – a non-Indigenous form of land management inspired by but not always accurately reflecting Aboriginal cultural burning knowledge and practices (e.g. see Russell-Smith et al. 2020) – is thus defined by the Australasian Fire and Emergency Services Authorities Council (2015: 9) as 'The controlled application of fire under specified environmental conditions to a pre-determined area and at the time, intensity, and rate of spread required to attain planned resource management objectives. It is undertaken in specified environmental conditions'. In the early 2000s, Australian Aboriginal cultural burning knowledge was even taken to California, USA, to develop prescribed burning regimes for the local conditions in an attempt to reduce the risk of future wildfires there (e.g. Kusmer 2020).

If Aboriginal and Torres Strait Islander fire-stick farming was, and in some parts of Australia continues to be, a widespread *cultural* practice, it must also have a history. Precisely how far back in time such a cultural history goes has long been of interest to Australian archaeologists and other Quaternary scientists and community members, but until recently the evidence has been difficult to interpret. Although researching the historical dimensions of cultural practices is the stuff of archaeology and cognate disciplines, how to investigate the deep-time history of a rich cultural tradition that does not involve stone tools, food processing or other kinds of activities that leave behind a material, archaeological record as conventionally defined presents a challenge. It is perhaps for this reason that while archaeologists across Australia have long been keenly aware of Aboriginal and Torres Strait Islander landscape burning practices, even to the point of claiming that Australia is not just a giant archaeological site but that the entire landscape is in effect a continental-size *artefact* given its ecological shaping through cultural fire (e.g. Jones 1969: 225), no archaeologist and very few palaeoecologists have ever undertaken an 'archaeology of fire-stick farming'. So how to go about doing this?

The answer is one that archaeologists, palaeoecologists and Indigenous communities are already well familiar with: transdisciplinary research. In this case, the 'site' of interest is the landscape, and the analysed 'artefacts' are the transformed vegetation communities, deposited ash and charcoal particles, and heat-altered sediments. The evidence does not relate just to a single, small location where people camped, painted, performed rituals and ceremonies or left individual tools or food remains, for example, but to much larger terrains best understood as managed *estates*. Here the concept of 'estate' is of particular importance, for it is not just socially and politically neutral 'land', but rather relates to place as affiliated and cherished territory – place as kin – that is culturally, socially, politically and ontologically organised and regulated by laws and social conventions of inter-personal behaviour. The idea of place as kin will be developed further through the case studies of cultural burning among the Martu and Yanyuwa in Sections 2.1 and 2.2. Other examples abound through the full length and breadth of Australia. The Law of other Aboriginal communities also helps to illustrate the care for 'estates' using deep ecological knowledge of fire and its consequences. An extraordinary example comes from Warlpiri Country, in the Tanami Desert of central Australia. Here Warlpiri families hold deep knowledge of the relatedness of the land, fire and rain in a traditional *ngapa*-rain narrative, in which two young warriors light a fire to 'flush the kangaroos out of the bush'. The smoke from the fire then produces great clouds and promotes rain, which in turn extinguishes the fire (Holmes & Jampijinpa 2013). The knowledge embedded in Warlpiri narratives, including that particles from smoke can seed clouds and bring rain at particular times of the year, was actively applied by burning patches of Country when members of Warlpiri families wanted to generate rain, emphasising the experienced actions of people in shaping their culturally and socially constructed estates.

Much like the construction and use of monuments, whether they be mounds, barrows, cemeteries or skyscrapers, there are social rules and conventions by which fires are lit in the landscape. The fires themselves, the smoke and the burned patches of land in particular, signal that people are or had been there, engaging with the land. They also signal that people appropriately affiliated with the land, or others who infringe(d) upon it, were asserting their right or power to be and do things on Country. In Aboriginal and Torres Strait Islander Australia, cultural burns are not just a set of fire events, but rather an announcement of social presences and the carrying out of social duties and fulfilment of Law as handed down from the founding ancestral Spirit-Beings (see Sections 2.1 and 2.2). Accordingly, an archaeology of fire-stick farming is at once a revelation of the history of firing practices, an examination of subsistence practices, a historicising of socially, politically and cosmologically ordained landscape management practices and an investigation of the social and political technologies that announce the right to be in place and the social signalling of such emplacements.

There are, however, different kinds of fires in the landscape, not just controlled burns initiated and used by people; wildfires can also rage across the landscape. To effectively investigate and frame the deep history of cultural burning, we must have a way of separating the two in analyses. In cultural burning, people burn mosaics of relatively small patches of land at any one time, resulting in the creation of a patchwork of variably burned habitats and plant growth (e.g. Lullfitz et al. 2017). Such anthropic landscape burning practices are often also called 'cool' or 'cool season' burns, because the firing of managed landscapes is usually undertaken during the 'cool season' when moisture remains in the grass rather than during the peak of hot summers or of the dry season when fires could more easily get out of control and denude the land of vegetation, and the fauna that depend on it. They are also called 'cool burns' because they are regularly lit, keeping fuel loads and fire intensities low. Fires lit for cultural burning do not reach the tree canopy, remaining close to ground level and burning off 'ladder fuels' that would otherwise continue to grow until they linked the ground with the canopy. With their relatively low fuel loads, cool anthropic landscape fires do not usually develop into high-temperature, uncontrollable and vast wildfires that engulf whole forests and that reduce the environment to monolithic vegetation communities (e.g. Clark 2020; see also Gammage & Pascoe 2021). With these differences between cultural burns and wildfires and their respective vegetation communities comes the possibility of differentiating the palaeoecological signatures of different kinds of past fires. We explore these methods for how they can help tell the (hi)story of a place and its people in Section 3, but first we present two case studies that reveal what fire-stick farming was and is all about.

2.1 Landscape Burning Among the Martu of the Australian Western Desert

The Martujarra or Martu, denoting the network of linguistic communities whose word for 'people' is '*martu*' ('*jarra*' = 'to have'), are a group of Aboriginal peoples of the Great Sandy, Little Sandy and Gibson Deserts. These three distinctive arid zone bioregions are often collectively referred to as the 'Western Desert' cultural bloc. The Martu-*wangka* ('dialect named units') consists of speakers of Kartujarra, Kiyajarra, Kurajarra, Manyjilyjarra, Nyiyaparli, Putijarra, and Warnman. The arid ecosystems of Martu country have a rich and varied biodiversity across a landscape with more than 1,118 known and mapped water-holding rockholes, saltpans, soaks, springs and lakes, most of which are ephemeral (Bliege Bird et al. 2020; Jupp et al. 2015: 576).

Many Martu families had lived continuously in the desert until the 1960s, when they moved to small rural towns and cattle stations following long droughts and widespread depopulation of the desert (Bird et al. 2016a: S69). In the 1980s, they decided to return to their desert estates to better access the land and so that they could fulfil cultural responsibilities relating to customary Law; these being the social laws handed down to clans by the Ancestral Beings at the beginning of time, including religious duties on sacred land. Being on the land meant the fulfilment of responsibilities to keep Country healthy by ascribed kin members as destined by Law, and a renewal of landscape management practices and foraging economies.

Martu families continue to actively maintain Country today through cultural land management practices often referred to as 'caring for Country'. One of these practices is the cool season burns which Martu families initiate across a landscape of some 500,000 hectares, with around 360 fires of around 100 hectares lit each year (Bird et al. 2016a: S74). When Martu are away from their traditional lands and fail to burn Country, wildfires from lightning strikes eventually ravage the land and its cultural sites, fuelled by heavy accumulations of leaf litter, fallen branches, scrub and dense dry spinifex (Figure 1). When on Country, the Martu burn relatively small patches of vegetation, the burned patches also incidentally acting as fire-breaks for lightning fires. The Martu fires are closely spaced, averaging 969 ± 723 m apart, in contrast to the fires lit by lightning, which average 8.93 ± 11.41 km apart (Bliege Bird et al. 2016: 221). We will return to this

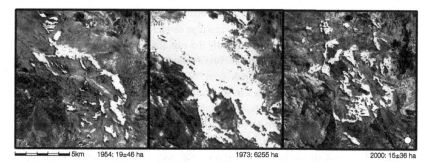

5km 1954: 19±46 ha   1973: 6255 ha   2000: 15±36 ha

Figure 1 Extent of fires (white) in the Yulpul region. Left: in 1954, when Martu were present and foraged on Country. Centre: in 1973, seven years after all Martu had left the region. Right: in 2000, after the return of Martu on Country in 1985, since when hunting and burning resumed. Remote sensing analysis performed by Rebecca Bliege Bird (from Bliege Bird et al. 2016: fig. 9.2).

point in what follows, for it can be an important consideration when trying to track the deep-time history of cultural burns versus wildfires through the methods of Quaternary science.

While it may be tempting to view Martu landscape burning practices through an environmental lens, it is in reality a deeply social practice that requires an understanding of Martu world views and social organisation. Burning is done by people, and people organise themselves socially, and on the ground, by how they understand the world to operate and through the social conventions and expectations of those world views. The activities that take place on the ground and that affect the physical environment are never devoid of social structure and cultural meaning.

In Martu cosmology, people obtained their languages, dances, songs, sacred sites, fecundity and the laws by which life is to be cared for from the *manguny* Dreaming (popularly known as 'Dreamtime') Ancestral Beings in *jukurrpa*, the Dreaming (for a classic discussion of Aboriginal concepts of 'The Dreaming', see Stanner 2011). Some are *tjilkannatja* or travelling beings that journeyed through the land connecting places one to the other, and others are *ngurantatja* or local beings tethered to individual places (see Cane 2021; Tonkinson 1978). 'Human-like, yet larger than life and gifted with superhuman magical powers, these beings hunted, gathered, and interacted much of the time in similar ways to the living today', writes Tonkinson (1978: 15), '[b]ut in doing so they were also creating most of the land's distinctive forms'. He continues:

> Every Aboriginal group attributes a host of physical features in its territory to
> the activities of the Dreamtime beings, which are embodied in myths, songs,

and rituals. As they wander in their continual food quest, the Aborigines are surrounded constantly by what they regard as certain proof of the power and vitality of the creative beings. ... During the exploits of the ancestral beings, the vital life essence contained in their bodies and in everything they possessed remained undiminished, but not indivisible. For wherever they went, they left behind some of this fund of power, which later animated hosts of tiny spirit-children that were ultimately born as human beings. ... After their worldly activities came to an end, the Dreamtime beings 'died' and then changed into stones, other natural features, or celestrial bodies, never to be seen on earth again. However, the absence of any special beginning of the Dreamtime era is matched by the absence of any definite end. None of the ancestral beings is believed actually to have died. Their bodies disappeared or metamorphosed into some other form, but their spiritual essence remained. They and their associated spirits, some of which act as intermediaries between Dreamtime and human orders, retain ultimate control of plant, animal, and human fertility, and are thought to take a continuing interest in human affairs.

Each person in the Martu world has multiple totemic associations with their place of conception, birth, initiation, and paternal and maternal kin, with which they are fundamentally linked through the life-giving and life-sustaining Ancestral Beings who imbue individual places with their life forces (for further details, see Bird et al. 2019). But those connections also come with responsibilities to care for Country by carrying out the sacred rituals and maintaining the health of the landscape, and thereby the health of life itself. Caring for Country at once sustains and asserts the sacred design handed down to people by the Ancestral Beings as they shaped the land with their life essences. These sacred endowments are expressed today in everyday life, such as in the right and expectation to burn one's Country so as to keep it clean, extract its resources, and maintain its fecundity (see also Bird et al. 2016a for an expanded exposition of this point). There are also highly restricted acts, such as when secret knowledge is passed on to initiates in special, powerful places ('sacred sites'). Referred to as 'Law' (*yurlubidi*), this encompasses the sum of rules and expectations of life decreed by the Ancestral Beings and passed down from generation to generation, including how people should organise themselves socially to enable them to act appropriately towards each other, and to all places across the Martu landscape. As Tonkinson (1978: 14) notes, 'All will be well if only they live according to the rules laid down by the spiritual beings who created their universe.'

Each of the Martu language communities consists of 'a number of estate-groups whose members are normally dispersed in bands throughout and perhaps beyond its territory. ... The estate-group can be elusive to identify because its members never assemble en masse to the exclusion of other like groups' (Tonkinson 1978: 50–51; for contemporary data showing this, see Bird et al. 2019; Bliege Bird et al. 2016). As previously noted, a person can be a member of an estate-group in multiple ways, such as through their place of conception, birth, initiation or 'because of his or her father's membership of the estate-group (and through the mother to her natal estate, though this linkage is less often stressed)' (Tonkinson 1978: 51–52). However, while an *estate* relates mainly to the places a person 'belongs' to through their Dreaming or totemic affiliations, the area they regularly frequent in everyday life (the *range*, see Stanner 1965) is much broader:

> The estate is the traditional heartland of what is most often some kind of patrilineal descent group. It consists of a limited number of important waterholes and sacred sites to which the members of the group are intimately related through bonds that imbue them with strongly felt sentiments of attachment and belonging. Whereas the tie to the estate is primarily a religious one, the relationship of social groups to their range is principally economic. A range is the large area exploited by bands during the food quest, and it normally includes within it an estate which a majority of members of the bands concerned think of as their *manda* ('main place'). ... In the desert the ranges of neighbouring estate-groups invariably overlap, and it is possible for individuals to develop strong allegiances to more than one estate in the course of their lives, which further adds to the openness of local organization. (Tonkinson 1978: 50)

A person's estate(s) is referred to in Aboriginal English as 'Country', as in 'this is my Country'. Individuals retain strong emotional attachments to Country, including to totemic centres within their estates. As Tonkinson (1978: 18) concluded,

> Landforms weld the Dreamtime solidly to territory; song and dance provide the means by which communication with the spiritual realm is enhanced and reciprocity is guaranteed; the mythology reveals the nature of the founding design and of its creators; and totemic beliefs complete the synthesis by providing vital linkages between individuals, groups, specific sites, and ancestral beings. The resulting unity is fundamental, not incidental, to the Aborigines' cosmic order.

Being on Country and acting out daily activities such as burning Country, hunting and foraging across the full range of one's estate is also a fulfilment of cosmological duty to connect with places and maintain the cosmic order as ordained by the Ancestral Beings since the beginning of time.

2.1.1 Cultural Burning and Subsistence

Today, the Martu obtain between 25 per cent and 80 per cent of their plant and animal foods from the bush. Two broad forms of animal food extraction are practiced: hunting of small, burrowing animals on foot mainly by women and children with *wana* (digging sticks), and hunting of larger fauna (e.g. kangaroos, emus) mainly by men with guns and, these days to a lesser extent, with spears. On average, most Martu hunt and forage for food items three to four days a week (Bird et al. 2005).

Between 2000 and 2010, ecological anthropologists Douglas Bird, Rebecca Bliege Bird and their colleagues set out to measure how cultural burning affects the productivity of Martu lands, as it is commonly assumed to do by the term 'fire-stick farming'. They accompanied Martu foragers on 368 hunting and foraging trips totalling 1,605 forager-days of participant observation with >4,500 quantitatively recorded foraging-hours (see especially Bird et al. 2016a: S74–S75, 2019; Bliege Bird et al. 2013, 2016). The desert camps ('foraging groups') averaged 8.2 people whose ages ranged between three and seventy years (Bird et al. 2019: 103; see also Bird et al. 2005). When walking the desert landscape for food, Martu foragers routinely set fire (*waru*) to the older patches of spinifex (*Triodia* spp.) tussock grass, a spiky, resinous grass that grows in clumps or 'hummocks' in sandy soil, especially in Australia's arid and semi-arid landscapes. Spinifex hummocks typically spread to about 1-m height and 2-m width when fully grown, and offer excellent cover for small fauna such as the carnivorous marsupial Wongai Ningaui (*Ningaui ridei*), the Sandy Inland Mouse (*Pseudomys hermannsburgensis*), and burrowing fauna such as the Sand Goanna (*Varanus gouldii*), Greater Bilby (*Macrotis lagotis*), Crest-tailed Mulgara (*Dasycercus cristicauda*), Rufous Hare-wallaby (*Lagorchestes hirsutus*) and Boodie or Burrowing Bettong (*Bettongia lesueur*). The cultural fires typically burn out patches of land of around 5 km^2 before they die out, so that over a period of years a mosaic of variably burned terrain covers the landscape across multiple estates. The burning reduces the spinifex hummocks to ash, clearing the ground of vegetation and allowing the Martu who walk behind the fires to track small fauna through the prints they leave in the sand and ash as they escape the fires (Figure 2). The immediate effects of the fires can also cause larger animals such as Perentie (*Varanus giganteus*), Yellow-spotted Monitors (*Varanus panoptes*) and Common Brushtail Possums (*Trichosurus vulpecula*) to be flushed out (Bliege Bird et al. 2016: 214–215).

The mosaic pattern of the cultural burns leaves behind a diverse landscape which the Martu classify according to how long ago an area was burned, along with the plant re-growth that the burning regenerates. Following Martu terminology, *nyurnma* refers to a bare patch of ground that was very recently burned, *waru-waru* to an area that saw the growth of herbaceous plants following rain, *nyukura* to an area with mature herbaceous plants and *kunarka* to a fully re-grown spinifex landscape (Bird et al. 2005: 449). While recently burned *nyurnma* terrain will typically be denuded of vegetation growth, following the first signs of rain the desert landscape sees the emergence of significantly more

Figure 2 Martu custodians (from right to left) Nyalangka Taylor, Ngamaru Bidu, and Nyaparu Taylor burn a tract of spinifex grassland, following behind the flames to begin hunting for sand goanna (photo by Rebecca Bliege Bird, Parnngurr region, 2014).

diverse young-growth plant communities than in a *kunarka* spinifex landscape that has not been burned for years.

The burning of the landscape results in much finer-grained habitat mosaics with noticeably richer plant and animal food resources than unburned landscapes. The fires enhance the growth of fruits such as the Bush Tomato (*Solanum* spp.), roots and tubers including the Pencil Yam (*Vigna lanceolata*), nectar from the Desert Grevillea (*Grevillea eriostachya*) and seeds from grasses and woody plants such as Woollybutt Grass (*Eragrostis eriopoda*) and wattles (*Acacia* spp.), which can be ground into flour.

The *nyurnma*, the burned-out patches of land, are critical for efficient *wana* foraging ventures. *Wana* foraging returns increase from 541 ± 827 to 1,256 ± 675 kcal/foraging-hour as people encounter from one to two stages of successional patch diversity per hour of foraging. During the cool and dry months of May to August in particular, the burning of late successional vegetation increases the success of small animal foraging 62-fold, from 25 to 1,552 kcal/foraging-hour. Summer foraging is less efficient due to the masking effect of increased plant cover on animal tracks (Bliege Bird 2013: 5–6; see also Bird et al. 2005: 453–454). The staged cultural burning increases the patch diversity (or mosaic structure) of the environment: the more hunting, the finer the mosaic; the finer the mosaic, the more

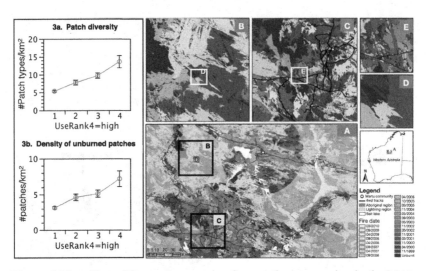

Figure 3 The effect of fire on the mosaic of vegetation succession in the Martu homelands. The stand ignition map shows the cumulative effect of both Martu and lightning fires between 2000 and 2010. Fires were visually detected and hand-digitised using a ration of Landsat 7 infrared bands 7 and 5. Light colours indicate more recent fires; dark shades indicate older fires. Regions across the study area are stratified into four categories of foraging intensity from 4,106 adult foraging hours observed between 2000 and 2010. Category 1 includes regions with 0–0.05 forager days/km^2; 2 = 0.06–0.25 forager days/km^2; 3 = 0.26–2 forager days/km^2; 4 = >2 forager days/km^2. A) The number of patches at different stages of vegetative succession/km^2 regressed by foraging intensity. B) Shows the number of old-growth patches (patches that remained unburned)/km^2 regressed by foraging intensity (after Bird et al. 2016b: fig. 3).

species diversity can be supported, particularly the species that are important for Martu (Bliege Bird et al. 2013, 2018) (Figure 3).

Doug Bird, Rebecca Bliege Bird and their team's research among the Martu specifically focused on systematically investigating whether regular cultural burning of the landscape indeed increased edible forage and improved hunting efficiency, as had been commonly assumed but never systematically investigated. Beyond this economic focus, they also crucially pointed out that cultural burning cannot be done by anyone, for Country is maintained by individuals and groups affiliated through ancestral estates, as described in Section 2.1. Land owners, and land users, manage Country following the blueprint laid down by the creation Spirit-Beings: these Ancestral Beings left not only their mark but also their power in the land, rendering it kin with their human offspring. Burning Country is thus done through relations of kin affiliation with ancestral estates. Accordingly, Martu keep close track of the individuals and foraging groups who burn patches of land, and in the ensuing months, years and decades following a fire, Martu individuals can recall who burned particular patches of land, and the social and territorial contexts of doing so.

During cultural burns, the tracked or flushed animals 'belong' to those responsible for the burns. Bird et al. (2005: 454–456) noted that '*wana* hunters failed to burn only on those occasions when they were hunting near ritual sites that proscribed burning or when members of the foraging party were not within their own estates', and 'women who hunt burrowed game have strong incentives to control moderate and repeated burns in order to immediately increase the probability of encountering game tracks and dens. As many Martu women reported, a *wana* hunt in a very large burn can be difficult to manage. Each burn (*nyurnma*) is "owned" by the individual(s) that fired it, and rights of access to the resources within that burn at least for that day are exclusive'. In particular, as women light fires while hunting Sand Goannas during the cooler months in the middle of the year, the physical landscape is transformed into small, variably burned patches of ground. Sand Goanna hunting with fire 'not only provides a reliable source of food', write Bliege Bird et al. (2016: 213), but it also 'brings people closer together in tight cooperative and sharing networks'. There is a social structure and moral ecology to hunting and foraging that is based on and promotes local understandings of existence – understandings of how the world operates – on social relationships and on burning and its subsistence benefits. By burning Country, both physically and socially, Martu inscribe the land that they have rights and responsibilities for, and for everyone to see: 'The most visible impact made by the Mardudjara on the land is the burning of grassland, a continuous practice' (Tonkinson 1978: 30; see also Bird et al. 2016a; Bliege Bird et al. 2008, 2012, 2018).

For Doug Bird and Rebecca Bliege Bird (personal communication 2022), five major conclusions stand out: (1) how profound Martu cultural burning is in shaping fundamental aspects of ecosystem function in the deserts (e.g. Bliege Bird et al. 2012, 2013, 2018); (2) how distinctive forms of social and ecological organisation emerge from the practice and consequences of cultural burning in Martu country (Bird et al. 2016a; Bliege Bird et al. 2013); (3) how settler colonialism ravaged cultural burning, causing 'trophic cascades' of devastation that appear to have contributed to the extinction of many native species (Bird et al. 2016a; Bliege Bird et al. 2008); (4) how Martu hunters reconstructed cultural landscapes in the 'homelands movement' (returning to Country after years of living in centralised townships), starting especially in the early 1990s (e.g. Bird et al. 2016); (5) how vital engaging with Country, including cultural burning, is today for remote-living Martu (Bliege Bird & Bird 2021; Bliege Bird et al. 2020).

Most anthropologists and archaeologists who have worked on cultural firing of the landscape have focused on either how burning has been used to extract or enhance food supplies from the environment, or how people relate to place-as-kin and all the social and emotional factors that come with that (e.g. Bird et al. 2005; Bradley 1995; Latz 1995; Lewis 1986). With their diverging research interests, few detailed studies have systematically ventured deeply into both aspects for any one Aboriginal community; the research in Martu country is exceptional in both its scope and depth of investigation. To further bring out this multi-dimensionality of cultural burning, we now discuss some deeper dimensions of the social and emotional ecology of burning through a different case study, that of the Yanyuwa of the Gulf of Carpentaria in tropical semi-arid northern Australia.

2.2 Cultural Burning among the Yanyuwa: Law and the Social, Emotional and Political Dimensions of Caring for Country

The Yanyuwa are a northern Australian Aboriginal group whose Country spans the lands and seas of the Sir Edward Pellew group of islands and the neighbouring coastal plains of the Australian mainland. Much of the social anthropological work with Yanyuwa has been undertaken by linguist and anthropologist John Bradley, whose work with Yanyuwa families is described in the following pages.

The Yanyuwa describe themselves as *li-anthawirriyarra*: as people whose spiritual source and culture is of the sea. As with other Aboriginal groups across Australia, the Yanyuwa recognise their origins in the Dreaming Ancestral Beings who gave them their language, dances, songs, kinship system, territory and Law or *narnu-yuwa*, a concept that signifies an existential decree handed down by the Ancestors from the beginning of time and into the future. 'The Law is the charter by which all beings in the environments are regulated', writes Bradley (1997: 145), and 'no part of the land and sea is without Law . . . Law can include all of the Spirit Ancestors associated with the islands, the names given to each locality, the food resources that can be found and the various rules and ways of acting' on the land and at sea. Understanding how Yanyuwa use fire to burn Country requires thinking through this Yanyuwa cosmology.

As outlined by Bradley (1997: 103–104):

> For the Yanyuwa their geographic landscape is a visible imprint and physical proof of the spiritual energies associated with their Spiritual Ancestors. These beings travelled across the landscape; they altered the landscape and left behind geographic features. . . . Such places mark episodes in the travel experiences of these Ancestors. When the Spirit Ancestors completed their travels they transformed themselves. Some became physical features such as rocks, hills, moon, stars and winds, whilst others became species of plants and animals. . . . The sharpest concentrations of the Spirit Ancestors' powers are found in such

marks: places where they created a land form, left an object behind, raised trees or entered the ground. These are the powerful places, in contemporary language, the sacred sites, the places where the most important knowledge resides, the knowledge is still used by the Yanyuwa people to assist in the maintaining of the life-order which is derived from the events of what they call the *yijan*[,] a word that generally translates into English as 'Dreaming'.

The *ngabaya* Ancestral Beings metamorphosed into the land and waters, handing over to the living the responsibilities of life and the caring of Country. Just as the *ngabaya* returned to the land in the Dreaming, maintaining their presence but distancing themselves from everyday life, so too do the spirits of dead people return to the land and waters, remaining on Country and interacting with the living in spirit form as 'shades', while remaining withdrawn from corporeal daily activities. But the Ancestral Beings nonetheless remain critically involved through the life essence and Law that they bequeathed to the living; the Ancestral Beings are the *li-ambirriju*, 'those who are in front', in contrast to the living who are *li-ngulakarringu*, 'those who come behind'. It is thus incumbent upon the living to care for Country, and upon whom 'all obligations fall of burning country, nurturing the family and maintaining the sanctity of the sacred places, just as the deceased did when they were living' (Bradley 1997: 7, 22).

A key concept in Yanyuwa philosophy is the notion of *nganji*, meaning 'kin' or 'relating to', in the sense that everything is existentially and contextually related in very particular ways. *Nganji* thus frames the fundamental relationships between the Yanyuwa and the plants and animals of Country (Bradley 1997: 9). In this cosmology, sea birds are 'kin to the fish, or hunters to dugong' and 'Dreaming-Spirit Ancestors or *yijan* are the source, the spring from which all possible relationships between human beings and the environment have originated' (Bradley 1997: 145). As the features of the land were created by the originary Ancestral Beings through their actions or by leaving behind parts of their bodies, they also imbue those places with their life forces, rendering the places themselves kin, as *nganji* to their living descendants. The result is also that the living hold responsibilities and deeply emotional ties to a Country that is kin (e.g. Bradley & Kearney 2009). Interacting with the landscape, such as through the burning of Country, is thus about interacting *in* and *as* the landscape, and more to do with acting responsibly to maintain the health, well-being and vitality of Country and all that comes with it, than about 'resource management' (Bradley 1997: 20).

In light of the land being kin, Yanyuwa social organisation is critical to the structure of human actions on the land and water. Yanyuwa individuals trace their ancestry through each of four patrilineages, their father's father, mother's father, father's mother's brother and mother's mother's brother, and each of these lineages is associated with particular rights and responsibilities (Bradley 1997: 140).

Each also relates to an unnamed moiety and named semi-moiety. The semi-moieties divide people, places, all living things and various phenomena such as rain, wind and fire into one of four named social groups: Wurdaliya, Wuyaliya, Rrumburriya and Mambaliya-Wawukarriya.

> Semi-moieties are categories which codify relationships of importance in ritual activity. . . . Semi-moiety categories have a pivotal role in land owner-ship. All land and sea has semi-moiety classification. . . . all people belonging to one semi-moiety are perceived as owning all land and sea with the same semi-moiety category. Whilst semi-moiety categories are used to express general notions of land ownership, there are within each semi-moiety a number of smaller patrilineal clans, or patriclans. It is these patriclans, along with people recruited from their mother's father, who make up the core people responsible for certain tracts of land and sea. (Bradley 1997: 142–144)

2.2.1 Ngimarringki *and* Jungkayi

Yanyuwa recognise two major social categories that cut across these kinship structures: *ngimarringki* (land owners, who are paternal descendants of the Spirit Ancestors of an estate) and *jungkayi* (guardians or managers of the land/water and of the knowledge that goes with it) (Bradley 1997: 161). Every tract of land and water has its *ngimarringki* and *jungkayi*, or land owners and guardians. The *ngimarringki* are 'those people whose fathers come from the country', and the *jungkayi* are 'those people whose mothers come from the same country'; 'The significance of that division is that the wants, needs, and responsibilities in relation to the land and ritual are apportioned between those who are either *jungkayi* or *ngimarringki*' of a place, writes Bradley (1997: 161). 'The *ngimarringki* role is paternally transmitted and comes to a person from his or her father, while the role of the *jungkayi* is transmitted from the mother's father. The effect of this system is that people are both *ngimarringki* for one area and *jungkayi* for another.' It is the *jungkayi* who are responsible for burning Country, as guardians of the land.

Among the Yanyuwa, as is the case also across Australia, fire is thus 'a social and cultural power as well as a biological and physical power' (Bradley 1995: 25). Here Country is burned during the very early stages of the dry season, when the grass still holds moisture from the earlier, wetter seasons. In Yanyuwa cosmology, the wet season is a time when the Rainbow Serpent is most active, when the cyclones and heavy rains occur. As the Rainbow Serpent is curtailed at the end of the wet season, the Black-Nosed Python takes over and the time for burning begins (Yanyuwa families & Bradley 2016: 3–6). People thus know Country not just for what it produces in terms of food and resources but more intimately for what has taken place there, for how those events can be connected to particular landscapes richly infused with powerful Spirit-Beings and ancestral presences, rights in customary Law to enter and ritually sing and perform activities in places, and for how people recall those events. The initiation of fires by the *jungkayi* signals 'looking after Country' by carrying out responsible land management and the fulfilment of social and sacred duties. Bradley (1995: 26) recounts Yanyuwa Elder Ida Ninganga lamenting the passing of the Old People and the regular burning of Country in 1986:

> Oh, all of the islands, they would once be burning, from north, south and east and west, they would be burning, the smoke would be rising upwards for days, oh it was good, you could see the smoke rising from here and also from Borroloola [the major residential town in the region], you knew where all the families were, it was really good, in the times when the old people were alive.

The fires may have 'cleaned' Country by removing overgrowth and leaf litter, and aided in foraging and hunting, but they also kept people in contact across long distances; the fires enabled people to keep track of who was where in the knowledge that families maintained the health of their part of Country in the 'proper way'. Burning Country thus also serves as social presence, connectivity and reassurance and to monitor past, present and required actions. People would see and remark among themselves how Country was occupied, and point out that 'such and such' was on Country, caring for it in appropriate ways according to the Law of the land, as passed down through the generations. That 'proper way' is not just technological know-how of where and when to burn but defined by kinship, political will, cultural expectation and Law. As Bradley (1995: 28) stresses,

> For the Yanyuwa the burning of country is an important way of demonstrating a continuity with the people who have died, their ancestors, or *li-wankala*, the 'old people'. The spirits of these people are said still to inhabit the landscape; they still hunt, sing, dance and are said even to still burn the country. Indeed it is spoken by the contemporary old people that before the coming of the white people, the spirits of the deceased kin would set fire to the country themselves for hunting, and up until quite recently, country that was burnt was left for several days so the spirits of the deceased could hunt first. ... As one old Yanyuwa man has commented, 'This is the most important thing, to burn the country, to burn the bones of the animals we catch on the country ... to make the smoke come up, so we smell it and they [the spirits] smell it.'

For Yanyuwa, the importance of burning Country is thus integrated into the philosophy of being:

> It is said that one part of a person's spirit leaves the body and travels to the spirit land in the east. As the spirit comes closer to the spirit land it is approached by a number of crows with long sharp digging sticks who intend

to kill the spirit by piercing it many times. These crows call out to the spirit, 'Go away from here, when you were alive you called us the eaters of faeces, and you chased us from your camp!' As the crows get closer, the 'followers of the fires over country', the hawks and falcons, come forward with their fighting sticks. Shouting out, they fight off the crows, calling out, 'Leave that spirit, when it was a living person, it burnt the country for us, it enabled us to eat.' The hawks and falcons thereby achieve for the spirit its entry into the spirit world. Thus even at death the obligations incumbent on people to burn country become a focus. (Bradley 1995: 29)

2.2.2 Burning as Cosmological-Political Inscription of the Landscape

As previously noted, it is the *jungkayi* of a place that has the right to burn Country or that can give permission for others to do so. During the earliest stages of the dry season in March and April, the cool dry season that Yanyuwa call *a-mardu* when occasional rains still fall, individuals 'begin to approach the people who are related to various tracts of country through their mothers, to seek permission to burn' (Bradley 1995: 29, 1997: 116–117). As Bradley (1995: 30–31) further explains, 'Smoke from country that is burning tells the observer that everything is good, the people on that land are well and doing what is required of them' according to Law.

> The burning of country requires method, not just in relation to when and how the country will be burnt, but also in relation to who will burn, hunt and gather. . . . It is important to note that burning country is not just fire, smoke and blackened vegetation. Firing country involves people who have ways of interpreting their place within the environment where they live, on the country they call home. Their relationship with fire at its most basic is as a tool, but fire is also related to events associated with the past and the future, events which to the outsider may not be considered that important, but to the indigenous community are very important. Fire, then, can be seen to be a part of an ecology of internal relations; no event occurs which stands alone. An event such as the lighting of country is a synthesis of relationships to other events

Fire and smoke inscribe Country socially, politically and cosmologically and enable people to immerse themselves as proper *jungkayi*, guardians of the land (for a detailed account of Country as kin among the Yanyuwa, see Bradley & Yanyuwa families 2022).

2.3 Investigating the Deep-Time History of Cultural Burning

If archaeology is about working out what happened in the past – the (hi)story of cultural practices examined via material evidence such as produced through the methods of Quaternary science – then it is about investigating through these methods how people inhabited and dwelled in their landscape (*sensu* Ingold 2000; Thomas 2008). How, then, can we do a landscape archaeology of the kind that would reveal deep-time historical details of landscape burning as practiced by Aboriginal groups such as the Martu and Yanyuwa?

We now explore in Section 3 ways of investigating the practice of cultural burning through colonial art. Then, in Section 4, we detail a number of recently developed techniques that have been used to investigate the history of cultural burning over timeframes that extend over thousands of years. We will then present in Section 5 a regional case study that puts some of these Quaternary methods into practice, as a way of illustrating how deep-time cultural fire histories can be revealed.

2.4 Further Readings

Bird, D. W., Bliege Bird, R., Codding, B. F. & Taylor, N. (2016a). A landscape architecture of fire: Cultural emergence and ecological pyrodiversity in Australia's Western Desert. *Current Anthropology* 57, Supplement 13: S65–S79. https://doi.org/10.1086/685763.

Bliege Bird, R., Codding, B. F. & Bird, D. W. (2016). Economic, social, and ecological contexts of hunting, sharing, and fire in the Western Desert of Australia. In Codding, B. F. & Kramer, K. (Eds.), *Why Forage?: Hunters and Gatherers in the Twenty-First Century*, pp. 213–230. Albuquerque: University of New Mexico Press.

Bliege Bird, R., Taylor, N., Codding, B. F. & Bird, D. W. (2013). Niche construction and Dreaming logic: Aboriginal patch mosaic burning and varanid lizards (*Varanus gouldii*) in Australia. *Proceedings of the Royal Society B* 280: 20132297. https://doi.org/10.1098/rspb.2013.2297.

Federation of Victorian Traditional Owner Corporations (no date). *The Victorian Traditional Owner Cultural Fire Strategy*. https://gunaikurnai .org/wp-content/uploads/2021/07/Victorian-Traditional-Owner-Cultural-Fire-Strategy-ONLINE.pdf.

Fletcher, M.-S., Hall, T. & Alexandra, A. (2021b). The loss of an Indigenous constructed landscape following British invasion of Australia: An insight into the deep human imprint on the Australian landscape. *Ambio* 50: 138–149. https://doi.org/10.1007/s13280-020-01339-3.

Gammage, B. (2011). *The Biggest Estate on Earth: How Aborigines Made Australia*. Melbourne: Allen & Unwin.

Garde, M., Nadjamerrek, B. L., Kolkkiwarra, M. et al. (2009). The language of fire: Seasonality, resources and landscape burning on the Arnhem Land

Plateau. In Russell-Smith, J., Whitehead, P.J. & Cooke, P. M. (Eds.), *Culture, Ecology and Economy of Fire Management in North Australian Savannas: Rekindling the* Wurrk *Tradition*, pp. 85–164. Melbourne: CSIRO. www .publish.csiro.au/pid/6056.htm.

Jones, R. (1969). Fire-stick farming. *Australian Natural History* 16(7): 224–228.

Lewis, H. (1986). Fire technology and resource management in Aboriginal North America and Australia. In Williams, N. & Hunn, E. (Eds.), *Resource Managers: North American and Australian Hunter-Gatherers*, pp. 45–67. Canberra: Australian Institute of Aboriginal Studies.

Rose, D. B. (Ed.) (1995). *Country in Flames*: *Proceedings of the 1994 Symposium on Biodiversity and Fire in North Australia*. Darwin: North Australia Research Unit, Australian National University.

Russell-Smith, J., McCaw, L. & Leavesley, A. (2020). Adaptive prescribed burning in Australia for the early 21st Century – context, status, challenges. *International Journal of Wildland Fire* 29(5): 305–313. https://doi.org/ 10.1071/WF20027.

Stanner, W. E. H. (2011). *The Dreaming and Other Essays*. Collingwood: Black Inc. Agenda.

Tonkinson, R. (1978). *The Mardudjara Aborigines: Living the Dream in Australia's Desert*. New York: Holt, Rinehart and Winston.

Yanyuwa families & Bradley, J. (2016). *Wuka nya-nganunga Li-Yanyuwa Li-Anthawirriyarra: Language for Us, the Yanyuwa Saltwater People – A Yanyuwa Encyclopaedia* Volume 1. North Melbourne: Australian Scholarly.

3 Reading Past Cultural Burning Through Colonial Art

Over recent years, a growing number of scholars have looked to landscape paintings and drawings – often the only surviving visual records of a physical landscape at a particular point in its history – for environmental, historical and cultural information they may hold (e.g. Gaynor & McLean 2008). Works dating from the nineteenth century are particularly valuable for such interdisciplinary research because they were created at a time when sketching and painting directly from 'nature' was becoming more widely practiced, and when landscape painters were becoming increasingly aware of the relevance of the new developments in the natural and Earth sciences to their practices. Rather than continuing the seventeenth-century tradition of the classical 'ideal' landscape, European landscape painters of the later eighteenth and early nineteenth centuries became fascinated by volcanic and glacial phenomena, they understood the geological character of the rocks they portrayed, their cloud formations became meteorologically specific and, rather than the generic tree forms found in earlier landscape paintings, their trees became identifiable as oaks, elms or eucalypts. Their observations were made on the spot and recorded in pencil or pigment on paper. Landscape photography, which was still in its infancy and limited by the difficulties involved in the transport of the cumbersome equipment required, did not rival the observations made by artists on-site until much later.

In Australia, works dating from the late eighteenth and early nineteenth centuries are particularly valuable for the information they can convey about the physical landscape at the point or in the early years of British colonisation. Amateur or professional colonial artists, particularly those who travelled with explorers or on scientific expeditions, were often the first Europeans to see and record a particular location. Scholars have interrogated the archive of colonial Australian art for information about, for example, the water levels of crater lakes and coastal environments, forest densities, the prevalence of botanical species in specific regions and for evidence of past wildfires and Aboriginal cultural burning and land management practices (Bonyhady 2000; Gammage 2011; Hateley 2010; Pullin 2023).

This section offers some preliminary guidelines for the consideration of colonial art as a source of information about the physical landscape, in particular for evidence of cultural burning. It suggests some key introductory considerations for ensuring that conclusions reached are reliable, and that appropriate art-historical protocols are observed. The discussion is informed by the example of the Austrian born, European-trained landscape painter, Eugene von Guérard (1811–1901), a scientifically oriented and technically skilled artist who, between late 1852 and the late 1870s, made direct sketches during his extensive travels throughout the south-eastern colonies of Australia.

3.1 The Artist's Practice

When assessing whether a particular work is, or was intended to be, an accurate portrayal of the landscape, it is important to begin with an understanding of the philosophy underpinning the artist's practice, the role of contemporary aesthetic conventions in the pictorial construction of the work in question and the purpose for which it was produced. Landscape paintings are more than topographic depictions of a physical landscape or its ecologies; they convey, and are mediated by, human responses to a particular place or to 'nature' more generally. The composition, light and atmospheric effects and the inclusion or absence of people or animals will all play a part in the way that landscape is read. The presence or absence, for instance of Indigenous peoples or, alternatively, of

Europeans in a particular setting, will dramatically change how that landscape is interpreted and understood. The artist may have made compositional changes, adding or excluding landscape features in order to conform with contemporary aesthetic conventions. Typically, in the classical Western landscape painting tradition, foreground trees or landforms served to 'frame' and balance a composition and, by emphasising the foreground plane, heighten the sense of pictorial depth. Aesthetic ideals, such as the 'picturesque' and the 'sublime', had a profound influence in the late-eighteenth- and early-nineteenth-century Western art tradition, shaping the way artists and their audiences responded both to physical landscapes and landscape paintings. The picturesque aesthetic focused on the visual delight to be found in the irregular forms of the 'natural' landscape, while the sublime was experienced in response to the awe-inspiring, fear-inducing extremes of elemental nature – typically deep, apparently bottomless chasms, mountain peaks lost in mist or violent storms at sea. In the context of Western colonisation, the pastoral tradition, which celebrated the taming of nature in bucolic views of peaceful, settled and bountiful landscapes, had a particular role to play. The way a landscape was portrayed could reflect the patron's expectation: for example, the scale of a landholder's estate could be seemingly amplified by the breadth of the view, or the deliberate erasure of the visual presence of Indigenous people from the landscape could serve to endorse the squatter's 'rightful' claim to that land.

Even a cursory study of von Guérard's surviving works – sketchbooks, his extensively annotated drawings, paintings and lithographs – reveals the analytical and inquiring eye he brought to his studies of 'nature', and the degree to which he sought to look beyond the surface of the natural world and to understand its inner workings; he was an artist for whom detail and 'truth' were paramount. He belonged to a generation whose understanding of the natural world was profoundly shaped by the ideas of the brilliant German polymath, traveller and natural scientist, Alexander von Humboldt (1769– 1859). Humboldt had addressed landscape painters specifically in the second volume of his hugely popular *Cosmos*, urging them to paint 'Descriptions of nature ... with sufficient sharpness and scientific accuracy', together with 'the vivifying breath of the imagination' (Humboldt 1847: 438). Von Guérard formed close connections with the cohort of eminent German-speaking Humboldtian scientists and artists who settled in Melbourne in the early 1850s, and who included the botanist Ferdinand von Mueller and the geophysicist Georg von Neumayer. Humboldt's vision of art and science as complementary practices was realised in practice in 1862, when von Guérard travelled with Neumayer on a two-month expedition that culminated in an ascent of Mount Kosciuzsko (Pullin 2011: 246). Empirical observation, the fundamental premise of Humboldtian science, informed the methodologies of both men, with von Guérard using a finely sharpened pencil to record his observations in his sketchbook while the scientist measured physical phenomena with his barometer and theodolite.

An artist's ability to realise her or his aspirations will, of course, vary with the individual's technical skill and level of training. Von Guérard's exceptional ability to see and record the world in often minute detail began with his artist-father, Bernard von Guérard, a painter of portrait miniatures. Von Guérard later studied in the progressive school of landscape painting at the renowned Düsseldorf Academy. The practice of painting studies in the open air was central to the school's curriculum, and the drawings he made on an extended expedition through the volcanic Eifel region of western Germany in 1843 reveal his engagement with contemporary geological research (Pullin 2009: 6–33).

While von Guérard's sketches, drawings and paintings can generally be accepted as faithful records of the physical landscapes he portrayed, there are exceptions, and every work must be considered individually. One way to do this is to consider the role of a work within an artist's practice.

3.2 The Artist's Medium and Its Purpose

To assess whether a work is likely to be a direct or unmediated record of a particular location, it can be helpful to consider its place and purpose in the artistic process. A pencil or oil sketch made on the spot and specifically for the artist's own reference in the studio is likely to be accurate. As such drawings were not regarded as finished works of art, there was no need for the composition to be adjusted to meet pictorial conventions. As the nineteenth century progressed, works produced directly in the field were increasingly regarded as works of art in their own right.

To determine the extent to which a work created in the studio can be considered a reliable record of a physical landscape, it can be useful to compare the finished painting with the artist's on-site sketches. In von Guérard's case, this is usually possible as he was a prolific draughtsman and most of his Australian sketchbooks and loose drawings have survived. He carried small, pocket-sized sketchbooks on all his expeditions and larger, loose sheets of paper on most trips; occasionally, he painted oil sketches in the field. He used a finely sharpened pencil to record panoramic views and close-range detailed studies on the spot, many of which he worked up in ink and wash. In notes, written in English or old German, he recorded colours, light effects, rock types and the species of trees or plants depicted. In his Melbourne studio, he worked with the sketches and drawings made on the spot, transferring his observations to the canvas or paper (for formal 'presentation' drawings) or onto stone to be lithographed. Infrared imaging has revealed the meticulous level of detail in the underdrawing that lies below the layers of pigment of particular paintings. It seems that he used a system of strings to square up his canvases so that he could transfer the original drawing to the larger canvas, section by section, scaling it up appropriately as he progressed (Varcoe-Cocks in Pullin 2011: 30).

While von Guérard generally remained faithful to his on-site observations, changes were sometimes made in the studio. Typically, when working in the field, von Guérard would record the middle and background of a landscape with meticulous precision while the foreground was often loosely suggested in a few cursory strokes. He would resolve the details of the foreground in the studio according to the compositional requirements of the finished work, perhaps with the introduction of people, animals, a fallen log or a rock formation. Similarly, he often recorded the panoramic sweep of a landscape over two – or more – pages of his sketchbook. The transference of the panoramic drawing to the squarer format of the canvas required subtle and incremental adjustments in order to retain a sense of topographical accuracy. In some cases, a peak may be slightly heightened or its angle of incline steepened for dramatic effect. And, in a note to the unwary, there are just a few examples in von Guérard's oeuvre of studio works that are composites of two separate drawings, in some cases taken from different locations.

Virtually all of von Guérard's surviving sketches and drawings, and those of many landscape painters working in nineteenth-century Australia, are accessible in digital form on the websites of the State Library of New South Wales, Sydney; the State Library of Victoria, Melbourne; the National Library of Australia, Canberra; the National Gallery of Australia, Canberra and the Alexander Turnbull Library, Wellington, New Zealand. Care must be taken to ensure that each work discussed or reproduced is correctly documented with its full title, date, medium, dimensions (if helpful), and the collection in which it is held. This referencing will also enable the reader to understand the stage in the work's production that it relates to: that is, whether it was done in the field or in the studio, and whether it was copied from an earlier drawing.

Unlike paintings and drawings, artist's prints – etchings, engravings and lithographs – exist in editions of multiple impressions. Each impression is an original work of art. Prior to the founding of the National Gallery of Victoria in 1861, most people in nineteenth-century Melbourne could only see paintings at the rare public exhibitions held in the colony, or in one of the shop windows where artists' works were sometimes shown. Oil paintings were mostly locked away in private homes. Prints, which were far more affordable and more portable than paintings, could reach a much wider audience. The twenty-four colour lithographs von Guérard produced for his *Eugène von Guérard's*

Australian Landscapes between 1866 and 1868 could be purchased as a set, either bound in an album or unbound. His aim was to 'put before the public views from this part of the world that demonstrate the character of the Australian landscape faithfully and with truth to nature' (von Guérard 1870, cited in Pullin 2011: 25). He envisaged an Australian and a European market, and his hope that they would reach a scientifically informed audience was realised when the eminent German geologist Ferdinand von Hochstetter (1829–1884) presented 'Eugène von Guérard's Australian Landscapes' in an address to the members of the Geographical Society in Vienna in 1870.

As recent research has shown, von Guérard's lithographs are repositories of valuable information, some of it registered serendipitously. With his eye for detail and commitment to accuracy, he recorded information that twentieth- and twenty-first-century researchers have been able to interpret but which he may not have understood. In June 1856, when he visited Budj Bim (Mount Eccles), he could not have been aware of the significance of the necks or channels of open grassland that he saw and recorded in the drawing for his lithograph, *Crater of Mount Eccles, Victoria* (Figure 4). Framed by belts of trees, these open channels are like corridors that lead down to (and back from) the water: they are, as Bill Gammage recognised in 2011, the result of the strategic land

Figure 4 Eugene von Guérard (artist) and Hamel & Ferguson (printer), *Crater of Mount Eccles*, Victoria 1867, colour lithograph, 50.6 × 68.7 cm. Plate 16 from *Eugéne von Guérard's Australian Landscapes* 1866–1868 (courtesy of National Gallery of Victoria, Melbourne).

management practice of cultural burning of the landscape undertaken by Gunditjmara to attract and hunt game (Gammage 2011: 47). The artist's expressed conviction that his work would be 'of greater value' to the future than works 'which can be equally well taken for a misty English or Australian landscape' (von Guérard 1870) has here, it seems, been borne out by history.

Evidence of cultural burns can be found in many of von Guérard's paintings, drawings and lithographs. In one of his earliest and most important Australian paintings, *Tower Hill* 1855 (Figure 5), the apparently arbitrary areas of relatively open grassland that appear on the otherwise densely vegetated slopes of the scoria islands in the centre of the painting testify to the cultural burning practiced by the Worn Gundidj at this location, possibly within the previous fifteen to twenty years. The scattering of juvenile trees signals the imminent return of the slopes to their forested condition. In the 1960s, this painting was famously used as a reference for the revegetation of this botanically and geologically significant lake-filled nested caldera, following its near-complete environmental destruction in the later nineteenth and twentieth centuries (Bonyhady 2000: 336–366). The work was commissioned in 1855 by the conservation-minded local pastoralist, James Dawson, who campaigned for the preservation of this unique place. However, by the end of the century, Koroitj (Tower Hill) had been devastated by the combined effects of wildfires, clearing, grazing, infestations of introduced species and feral animals, and the lake had become an outlet for urban waste. Neither Dawson nor von Guérard could have imagined the role that the painting that they had brought into

Figure 5 Eugene von Guérard, *Tower Hill* 1855, oil on canvas, 68.6 × 122.0 cm. Warrnambool Art Gallery, Victoria (courtesy of Warrnambool Art Gallery).

existence, as patron and artist, would play in its restoration: it is a compelling example of the power of colonial art to inform the present.

With his interest in the natural sciences, his philosophical commitment to accurate and detailed observation and the technical skills to realise his vision, von Guérard is an ideal artist to consider when consulting colonial art for evidence of past cultural burning. However, the works of many other colonial artists, both professional and amateur, have the potential to inform and extend research. Their works can be accessed on the websites of Australia's national and state libraries and art galleries. New and more nuanced understandings of cultural burning and land management practices will undoubtedly emerge as researchers from diverse disciplines bring their expertise to bear on what is the rich archive of colonial Australian art.

3.3 Further Readings

Bonyhady, T. (2000). *The Colonial Earth*. Carlton: The Miegunyah Press, Melbourne University.

Gammage, B. (2011). *The Biggest Estate on Earth: How Aborigines Made Australia*. Melbourne: Allen & Unwin.

Pullin R. (2018). *The Artist as Traveller: The Sketchbooks of Eugene von Guérard*. Ballarat: Art Gallery of Ballarat.

Pullin, R. (2023). Eugene von Guérard on GunaiKurnai Country 1860–1861: Reading the story of fire in his depictions of the landscape. In Buettel, J., David, B., Mullett, R. et al. (Eds.), *Fires in GunaiKurnai Country: Landscape Fires and their Impacts on Aboriginal Cultural Heritage Places and Artefacts in Southeastern Australia*, pp. 36–52. Oxford: Archaeopress.

4 Cultural Burning in the Quaternary Record: Scientific Approaches, Methods and Applications

Aspirations of research into past fire regimes and cultural burning can, and usually do, involve much longer time frames than the period since colonial settlement in the past few hundred years. In many parts of the world, oral histories can take us so far back in time, but social memories fade and can change in the face of new experiences and new perspectives. A range of Quaternary science methods have thus been developed in recent years, to reveal demonstrable and testable evidence of past cultural burning. These palaeoecological methods are independent of the archaeological record itself (in the sense of buried artefacts and stratigraphies), although the ash and charcoal and sediments produced through cultural burning can rightfully be themselves considered 'artefacts', in the sense that they are produced through the actions of people, through human skill. The results of such analyses can usefully be compared to the archaeological records of settlements and artefact distributions to better understand the timing and role of cultural burning across the landscape.

Six major palaeoecological methods are currently being used to investigate the deep-time history of cultural burning:

- Charcoal accumulation rates in lake/wetland sediments as an indicator of past fire activity
- Charcoal peak analysis to reconstruct the past frequency of fire episodes
- Fourier-transform infrared spectroscopy (FTIR), hydrogen pyrolysis and charcoal reflectance to estimate past fire temperatures
- Charcoal morphology and isotopic composition to examine what plants were being burned
- Fire-scar studies to reconstruct fire extent and frequency
- Vegetation reconstructions of cultural landscapes using pollen data.

We describe each method in Sections 4.1 to 4.7, noting that many studies integrate several of these approaches.

4.1 Charcoal Accumulation Rates (Biomass Burned)

Charcoal particles deposited in the sediments of lakes and wetlands are one of the most widely used methods for exploring fire histories. Charcoal has the advantage of being chemically inert, so legacies of past fires persist in sediments almost indefinitely. The overall amount of charcoal deposited in a lake or wetland during a given period is related to the amount of biomass that has been consumed by fire in the surrounding catchment (Ali et al. 2012). This allows researchers to use charcoal accumulation rates to reconstruct the amount of biomass burned (BB) by fire in the past (Figure 6).

Charcoal accumulation rates depend on excellent chronological control so that sedimentation rates can be accurately determined. Poor dating may lead to erroneous conclusions about the timing, frequency and magnitude of BB. Charcoal accumulation is also influenced by local site factors, such as the ability for charcoal particles to enter the lake or wetland, which can depend on erosion, vegetation density and catchment hydrology as well as weather conditions at the time of fire (Whitlock & Larsen 2001). To account for these site-based differences, researchers have devised a number of methods to standardise charcoal accumulation data and allow comparisons between sites (e.g. z-score transformation: Power et al. 2008). Some of these methods involve the use of multiple charcoal records from various sites within a specific geographic area to

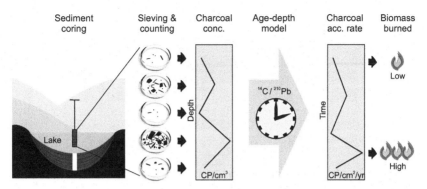

Figure 6 The process for estimating the amount of biomass burned in a past landscape from charcoal particles preserved in lake and wetland sediments. A sediment core is collected, representing a timeline of environmental change for the surrounding area. Charcoal particles are then extracted from the sediment using sieving and chemical treatments. Particles are counted to determine the charcoal concentration for each sample. Using an age-depth model, the rate of charcoal accumulation can be estimated. Low charcoal accumulation rates mean low levels of biomass burned, whereas high rates reflect high levels of biomass burned.

reconstruct a regional trend of biomass burning (Figure 7; e.g. Blarquez et al. 2015; Marlon et al. 2013). Although such studies are common and reveal interesting trends, the precise relationship between charcoal and BB is not well understood in most landscapes because of a lack of well-designed calibration studies.

In Australia as elsewhere, human modification of the fire regime is thought to date back tens of thousands of years (e.g. Clark 1983; Head 1989; Kershaw 1974; Singh & Geissler 1985). Researchers have found it difficult to differentiate cultural burning from wildfires over these long timescales from biomass-burned data. Some of the most common tools for reconstructing fire history (such as z-score transformation) are unable to provide a fair evaluation of cultural burning's history, given that they average charcoal data of variable quality from multiple sites representing vastly different environments and apply a statistical transformation that distorts the charcoal signal at the expense of local variation (McMichael et al. 2021). The poor integration of archaeological data into fire history studies has also been highlighted (Snitker et al. 2022). Regardless of the research design or theoretical framework adopted, 'biomass burned' may not be the best indicator of cultural burning, given that such fires typically consume little biomass compared to wildfires. For example, cultural

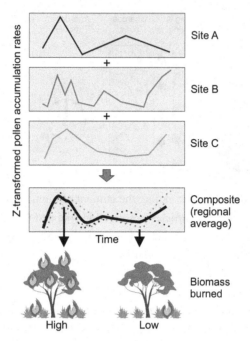

Figure 7 Combining multiple charcoal records into a regional trend of biomass burned. Charcoal accumulation rates are statistically transformed (z-scores) prior to averaging to aid comparison.

burning does not usually burn trees or tree canopies, remaining lower to the ground and affecting understorey shrubs and grasses of low biomass. Cultural burning has a nuanced, local signature that has been successfully identified in more targeted studies.

4.2 Charcoal Peak Analysis (Fire Frequency)

In some places, changes in fire frequency may be a more effective signal of past cultural burning than the overall levels of biomass burning, because the latter are largely indicative of the biomass available for burning, and therefore of environmental conditions, rather than how often fires occur. Methods for reconstructing fire frequency rely on the recurrence of distinct charcoal peaks in sediments (Higuera et al. 2009). Peak analysis can be applied to suitable charcoal data using a dedicated R package (Finsinger & Bonnici 2022). To ensure no fire episodes are missed, charcoal must be sampled contiguously through the entire sediment sequence at high temporal resolution, so that each sample represents only a few years and no fire events are missed (Figure 8). Using this approach, Theden-Ringl (2018) demonstrated

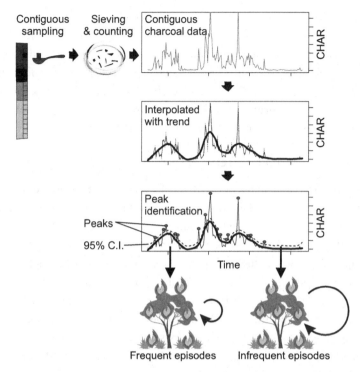

Figure 8 Estimating past fire frequency using charcoal preserved in sediments. Charcoal is sampled contiguously so that no fire events/episodes are missed. The data are then interpolated to even time steps and a smoother is added to model the long-term trend. Any peaks above the 95% confidence intervals are identified as fire events/episodes. The recurrence of these events/episodes through time helps to reconstruct past fire frequency.

how fire frequency in high-elevation ecosystems in south-eastern Australia was closely linked to the occupation history of neighbouring archaeological sites. The highest fire frequencies coincided with periods of densest occupation, in terms of the number of occupied sites. The temporal pattern of burning and occupation differed between three neighbouring catchments, suggesting a highly localised and specialised pattern of burning that cannot be explained by large-scale wildfires, although the latter also occurred infrequently in the three records.

Adeleye et al. (2021) likewise found that the Holocene occupation history of the Bass Strait islands (between Tasmania and mainland Australia) was reflected very clearly in changes in fire frequency but had no relationship with BB. This suggests that the way the landscape was shaped by people through fire varied through time as populations changed; we will return to this case study in

Section 5. The application of fire frequency studies is limited to areas where there are suitable sediments, preferably undisturbed organic sediments with enough sedimentation to allow individual fire events to be pinpointed. Routine chemical treatments used in charcoal sample processing may preferentially remove charcoal particles from low-intensity fires (Constantine & Mooney 2021), which could mean that evidence for low-temperature cultural burns has been underestimated or overlooked in previous research.

4.3 Fire Temperature Indicators

The methods described in Sections 4.1 and 4.2 relate to the quantity of charcoal particles accumulated in lake and wetland sediments, but there are considerable insights to be gained from analysing the chemical properties of the charcoal particles themselves. The reflectance of charcoal particles changes according to the temperature at which fuel was burned, and this characteristic has been used to assess fire temperatures from large charcoal pieces found in archaeological sites (e.g. McParland et al. 2009). Fourier-transform infrared spectroscopy allows reflectance spectra to be obtained from the microscopic charcoal fragments typically encountered in Quaternary sediments.

Gosling et al. (2019) used an experimental approach to test how FTIR spectra differed in plant material combusted at different temperatures (Figure 9). They showed that low, medium and high temperature fires could be confidently inferred from FTIR spectra and used this to infer past fire intensity in Ecuador (Gosling et al. 2019). Subsequent research has confirmed the ability of FTIR spectra to infer broad temperature ranges from charcoal particles from important plant species in South Africa (Maezumi et al. 2021) and Australia (Constantine et al. 2021). The FTIR spectra are not always easy to interpret due to the relatively poor preservation of charcoal produced at low temperatures and diagenic chemical processes within the sediment that can obscure the fire temperature signal. Despite its drawbacks, FTIR has great promise as a tool to track the timing and extent of past cultural burning and several research programmes are underway internationally. In Australia, some of these research projects are being undertaken in collaboration with Indigenous communities who are interested in finding out about the deep-time history of cultural burning by their ancestors.

4.4 Fuel Composition in the Past

The physical form of charcoal particles can also reveal something of the vegetation being burned, as well as of the fire itself. For example, sedimentary charcoal assemblages made up of small twigs and leaves are likely to be

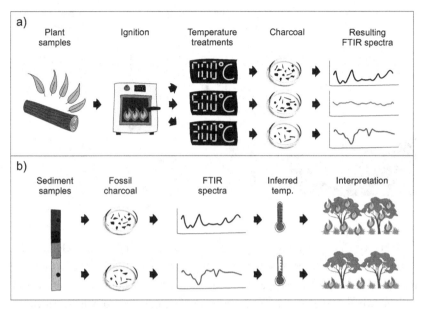

Figure 9 Fourier Transformed Infrared Spectroscopy (FTIR). a) calibration relies on igniting plant samples at different temperatures and measuring the FTIR spectra of the charcoal produced. b) reconstruction relies on extracting and measuring the FTIR spectra of fossil charcoal and using the calibration data to infer past fire temperature and, by extension, the prevalence of 'cool' cultural burning.

products of relatively cool fires, whereas woody charcoal might be indicative of hotter fires. At the microscopic level, charcoal morphology has been defined in various studies and allows researchers to differentiate charcoal particles from woody plants such as trees and shrubs from elongated charcoal particles that derive from burning grasses and sedges (Figure 10; Mustaphi & Pisaric 2014; Rehn et al. 2022; Umbanhowar & McGrath 1998). Another approach is to use carbon isotopic analysis to find out whether the charcoal came from plants with a C_3 or C_4 photosynthetic pathway, potentially discriminating between savanna grasses (which photosynthesise using the C_4 pathway) and most other plants (which use the C_3 pathway; Rehn et al. 2022).

These studies of past fuel composition, if conducted at appropriate spatio-temporal resolution and combined with pollen and charcoal data (Bird et al. 2019), have the potential to illustrate how cultural burning targeted different types of vegetation at different times, perhaps even to the level of understanding the fuel behind individual fire events. There is still much work to be done in linking charcoal morphology to fuel sources (vegetation) and fire characteristics

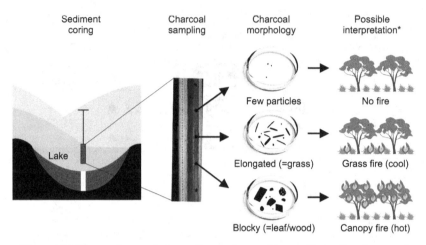

Figure 10 Charcoal morphology. Grass charcoal has a distinctly elongated shape, allowing researchers to reconstruct the contribution of grassy fuels to past fires. In certain landscapes, the ratio of grassy to woody/leafy fuels could indicate whether the fires were canopy or understorey fires, or whether areas of grassland or forest were being burned.

in a quantitative way. The trends can be interpreted as relative changes in fuels, but precisely how the abundance and composition of fuels in the surrounding landscape is reflected in charcoal assemblages is a matter for further research and calibration (e.g. Aleman et al. 2013).

4.5 Fire-Scar Studies

Fire-scar studies have proved to be exceptional sources of information on past cultural burning, especially for their high temporal and spatial resolution (Figure 11). North America is particularly rich in fire-scar data, due to the prevalence of suitable tree species (fire-surviving conifers with annual growth rings). Multi-disciplinary studies like that of Larson et al. (2020) provide detailed, annually resolved fire histories that are carefully situated in their cultural and historical contexts. They show how today's landscapes of high conservation value are in fact culturally formed landscapes; hence, current policies that exclude fire and other cultural practices are inappropriate in such places.

Another example is an exploration of spatial and temporal burning patterns in Arizona, showing how burning differed on Indigenous and non-Indigenous managed lands and between different land-uses within these areas (Whitehair et al. 2018). The fine spatial scale and high temporal resolution of the study design allowed researchers to accurately map the extent of past fires and to then

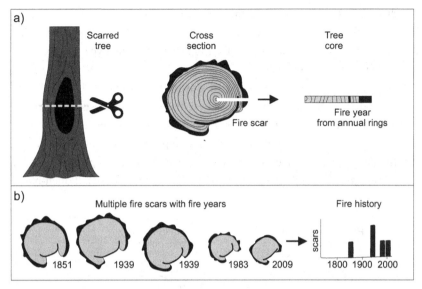

Figure 11 Fire scars. a) in appropriate trees, fire scars can be precisely dated by counting annual growth rings. b) by putting together the dates of fire scars from various trees, a fire history for a particular cultural landscape can be reconstructed.

tease apart climatic influences on past fires from factors such as land-use and pastoralism. Like the previous study, they showed how the nineteenth- and twentieth-century fire suppression was a marked departure from centuries of cultural burning. Fire-scar studies are limited to areas with suitable long-lived trees. As a result, they are lacking from parts of the world where such trees are absent or uncommon, including many parts of Australia.

4.6 Vegetation Reconstructions from Fossil Pollen

Cultural burning is also reflected in vegetation (i.e. fuel) structure and dynamics. The island of Tasmania provides numerous examples of how this can be achieved using fossil pollen evidence. For instance, Mariani et al. (2017) used pollen data and modelling to show how Tasmania's Holocene vegetation had developed into open landscapes of heathland, moorland and woodland rather than the dense rainforests that developed during previous interglacial periods. They linked this to Indigenous burning, which created diverse cultural landscapes with a large degree of openness. Romano and Fletcher (2019) found evidence for a divergence in vegetation trajectories between nearby sites in coastal Tasmania. They explained this divergence as a result of differences in human occupation and vegetation management, including cultural burning.

Fletcher et al. (2021b) analysed the vegetation change in Tasmania's Surrey Hills area after the arrival of colonial settlers in the 1830s, and concluded that the cessation of cultural burning was the trigger for fire-sensitive rainforest trees to invade areas of eucalypt savanna.

In a synthesis covering south-eastern Australia, Mariani et al. (2022) used pollen modelling (Figure 12) to show how the region's forests had grassier understoreys in the pre-European period. These grassy understoreys were maintained through regular cultural burning, but the suppression of Aboriginal cultural practices led to an invasion by shrubs that promote canopy fires through increased connectivity of fuels ('ladder fuels'). Pollen-based

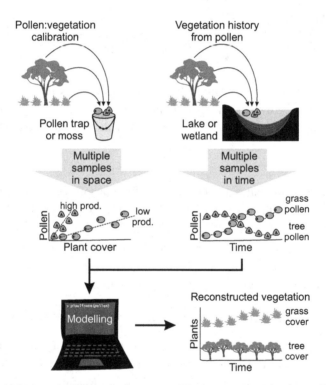

Figure 12 Vegetation cover in the past can be reconstructed using calibration and modelling. Calibration relies on multiple pollen samples and vegetation surveys collected in the present-day environment to determine the relationship between plants and pollen. In this way, high pollen producers (such as wind-pollinating species) can be downweighted compared to low pollen producers (like insect-pollinating species). Modelling allows a pollen record through time to be converted into reconstructed vegetation, potentially revealing cultural landscapes (e.g. Mariani et al. 2017, 2022).

studies are effective in demonstrating broad changes in vegetation at spatial scales from hectares to entire continents, but as yet they are unable to reconstruct finer-scale vegetation mosaics. Work is underway to develop realistic models of past vegetation mosaics using geographic information systems (Bunting et al. 2018) and in developing biomass estimates for ecosystems of the past to better understand the role of cultural burning in long-term forest dynamics (Knight et al. 2022).

4.7 Other Approaches and Perspectives

There are other approaches to reconstructing cultural landscapes and cultural burning, including historical paintings and maps, as demonstrated in Section 3 (Burch et al. 2020; Gammage 2011; Pullin 2023). These usually do not address deep-time beyond hundreds of years ago, though there are exceptions of successful integration of historical and palaeoecological data (e.g. Bickford & Mackey 2004; Bickford et al. 2008). Levoglucosan, an organic molecular marker, can provide insights into past fire regime changes on continental scales (Lopes dos Santos et al. 2013; Zennaro et al. 2015). When applied to lake sediments, levoglucosan- and charcoal-based fire histories exhibit broadly similar trends (Elias et al. 2001). Levoglucosan is considered a proxy for biomass burning at relatively low temperatures (<350 °C; Bhattarai et al. 2019), making it potentially a very interesting proxy for differentiating low-temperature cultural burning from higher temperature wildfires. However, unresolved issues surrounding levoglucosan degradation could diminish its indicator value in some regions (Häggi et al. 2021).

There is enormous scope for multiple perspectives to come together to form a more holistic view of past cultural burning in particular landscapes. Through respectful partnerships between Indigenous and Western knowledge-holders, new research horizons are likely to emerge based on hypotheses and experimental design that corroborate non-Western understandings of the world around us (Fletcher et al. 2021a). Some potential pathways could be, for example: (1) carefully designed analogue studies or targeted research at adjacent small sites as a support for the reintroduction of cultural burning in neglected cultural landscapes (e.g. Theden-Ringl 2018); (2) investigations of the plant functional traits, indicator species or vegetation structures that best reflect the nuances of cultural burning (e.g. Armstrong et al. 2021) and how these may manifest in palaeorecords; and (3) research partnerships that develop a collective understanding of what 'healthy Country' is today (e.g. Robinson et al. 2021) and how that may be recognised in the past. Obviously, different First Nations communities will have different research objectives and those should always be prioritised.

4.8 Closing Remarks

In today's landscapes, all fire has a cultural aspect. The way land is managed, lived in or cared for has an enormous bearing on fire regimes (Pausas & Fernández-Muñoz 2012), and the way land is understood is inherently cultural. Landscapes in the past were no different. It would be hard to find a single place on Earth where the imprint of past cultures is not reflected in the present. Scientific data can assist in unearthing the deep histories of places where this cultural imprint has been neglected or disrupted. In other places, scientific data can increase recognition of long-held cultural ties to the land, promoting conversations about ownership and stewardship rights where these have been denied. While scientific data from the past cannot provide prescriptions about how lands should be cared for, they do support alternative visions of how places can be and help describe how different peoples and cultures have imprinted themselves on the land and ingrained themselves into the living landscape.

4.9 Further Readings

Adeleye, M. A., Haberle, S. G., O'Connor, S. E., Stevenson, J. & Bowman, D. M. J. S. (2021). Indigenous fire-managed landscapes in Southeast Australia during the Holocene – New insights from the Furneaux Group islands, Bass Strait. *Fire* 4(17). https://doi.org/10.3390/fire4020017

Fletcher, M.-S., Romano, A., Connor, S., Mariani, M. & Maezumi, Y. (2021a). Catastrophic bushfires, Indigenous fire knowledge and reframing science in Southeast Australia. *Fire* 4: 61. https://doi.org/10.3390/fire4030061.

Maezumi, S. Y., Gosling, W. D., Kirschner, J. et al. (2021). A modern analogue matching approach to characterize fire temperatures and plant species from charcoal. *Palaeogeography, Palaeoclimatology, Palaeoecology* 578: 110580. https://doi.org/10.1016/j.palaeo.2021.110580.

Mariani, M., Connor, S. E., Fletcher, M.-S. et al. (2017). How old is the Tasmanian cultural landscape? A test of landscape openness using quantitative land-cover reconstructions. *Journal of Biogeography* 44: 2410–2420. http://dx.doi.org/10.1111/jbi.13040.

Mariani, M., Connor, S., Theuerkauf, M. et al. (2022). Disruption of cultural burning promotes shrub encroachment and unprecedented wildfires. *Frontiers in Ecology and the Environment* 20: 292–300. https://doi.org/10.1002/fee.2395.

Marlon, J. R., Bartlein, P. J., Daniau, A. et al. (2013). Global biomass burning: A synthesis and review of Holocene paleofire records and their controls. *Quaternary Science Reviews* 65: 5–25.

5 Historicising Cultural Burning through Buried Charcoal: Amount of Burned Vegetation and Recurrence Rates of Fire Episodes in the Furneaux Islands, Bass Strait, Australia

Let us now examine how the deep-time history of cultural burning can be investigated, through the example of one region of Australia, the islands of the Furneaux Group in Bass Strait, between the south-east Australian mainland and Tasmania.

5.1 Furneaux Group, Bass Strait

Bass Strait is a 240-km-wide seaway between mainland Australia and the large continental island of Tasmania to its south. Here lie the Furneaux Islands, a group of about 100 small islands ranging from 1,367 km^2 (Flinders Island) to less than 0.01 km^2 (e.g. Lady Barron Island) near the south-eastern corner of Bass Strait. During the Last Glacial Maximum, and beginning around 43,000 cal BP, the islands were connected to Tasmania and the Australian mainland by a land bridge, becoming severed through post-glacial sea-level rise sometime between 14,000 and 6,000 cal BP (Lambeck & Chappell 2001). Lewis et al. (2013) reviewed the patterns of eustatic sea-level rise for Australia, and while there are few data for Bass Strait for the Holocene, the timing of flooding can be estimated from the envelope of change for south-eastern Australia. The deepest parts of the channel between Clarke Island and Tasmania reach 60 m deep and would have been flooded at 13,500–12,750 cal BP, creating a funnel-shaped estuarine embayment. The average depth around the islands is between −30 and −40 m, which would have been inundated between 10,750 and 10,250 cal BP. The islands of today would have been entirely surrounded by water by 9,000 cal BP. Today the closest of the Furneaux Islands – Clarke Island – is separated from Tasmania by a 22-km sea crossing, and from there a series of short island hops each of less than 2 km leads to Flinders Island, itself 53 km away from the Tasmanian mainland.

The islands contain a range of ecosystems from temperate rainforest to *Eucalyptus* spp. forest and woodland and heathland, the respective distributions of which changed through time. To examine the history of these vegetation communities, fire regimes, and climate change, ten pollen and charcoal cores have been collected from lagoons on the two largest islands, Flinders Island (1,367 km^2, two cores) and Truwana (Cape Barren Island) (478 km^2, eight cores) (Adeleye et al. 2021). The Furneaux Islands have also received focused archaeological attention, with seven open and two rockshelter and cave sites with pre-colonial-period occupation deposits having been excavated and radiocarbon-dated (Anderson et al. 1996; Brown 1993; Orchiston & Glenie 1978; Sim 1991, 1994,

1998). To assess the history of fire on the landscape relative to the patterns of human occupation, we critically consider the details of both records side-by-side.

5.2 The Archaeology of the Furneaux Group

None of the Furneaux Group, or of the Kent Islands 50 km to the north-west, were occupied when European navigators and colonial settlers first came to the Bass Strait–Tasmanian region in the late 1700s and early 1800s (e.g. Baudin 1803; Flinders 1801, 1814), and the total absence of smoke from human activity on the islands puzzled the early colonial navigators (Flinders 1814: cxxxvi). Yet the presence of large numbers of archaeological deposits across the islands (e.g. Sim 1998: 45–50) shows that there was a time, deeper in the past, when Aboriginal peoples lived there. At Beeton Rockshelter on Badger Island, a small island of 12.42 km^2 located 12 km to the west of Flinders Island, Sim (1998) showed that people were camping at the site between 23,180 ± 1,280 BP (AA-15143, on emu eggshell) and 8,891 ± 136 BP (ANU-8750, on *Cellana solida* shell), calibrating to 24,731–30,030 cal BP and 9,194–10,083 cal BP, respectively (after Sim 1998: 70–86) (all calibrations of radiocarbon ages are given at 95.4 per cent probability, and were recalculated on Calib 8.20 using the SHCal20 curve for charcoal and emu eggshell, or Marine20 with a ΔR value of – 151 ± 79 for *Cellana solida* limpet shell and for muttonbird/shearwater (*Puffinus* spp.) bone). The deep cultural layers were sealed by a higher, younger layer of sand from a natural muttonbird rookerie, its rich *Puffinus carneipes*, *Puffinus griseus* and *Puffinus tenuirostris* bone deposit dating from 5,440 ± 110 BP (OZA 782) to 4,540 ± 90 BP (OZB 591), calibrating from 5,465–6,120 cal BP to 4,385–5,085 cal BP, respectively (Anderson et al. 1996; for matters relating to ΔR values, see Higham et al. 2005; Hua et al. 2020). There are no signs of people at Beeton Rockshelter after c. 9,500 cal BP until the early colonial period. Similarly, at Mannalargenna Cave on Prime Seal Island (12.20 km^2), 6 km to the west of Flinders Island, the 4.05-m-deep excavation revealed a sequence of occupational layers dating between 23,015 ± 210 BP (AA-13040, on charcoal) and 7,910 ± 270 BP (ANU-9023, on emu eggshell), calibrating from 26,599–27,740 cal BP to 8,185–9,423 cal BP, respectively (Sim 1998: 249–262; see also Brown 1993). Occupation in the cave ceased c. 9,000 cal BP, as Prime Seal Island became an island, just as it ceased at a similar time at Beeton Rockshelter as Badger Island also became an island.

On Flinders Island, by far the largest island in the Furneaux Group, the situation is slightly different. Here seven open archaeological sites – all marine shell-bearing sites, some also containing stone artefacts – have been radiocarbon-dated. At Palana on the northern end of the island, stone artefacts and concentrations of shell from food remains in dune blowouts indicate extensive cultural deposits. Charcoal associated with, or near, stone artefacts and shell from food refuse on old, partially buried palaeosols at two open sites, P12 and P13 in the Palana dunes at the northern end of Flinders Island, gave radiocarbon determinations of 6,520 ± 130 BP (SUA-642) and 7,150 ± 135 BP (SUA-641) (site P12) and 9,890 ± 175 BP (SUA-640) (site P13) for the occupation palaeosol, calibrating to 7,031–7,615 cal BP, 7,666–8,275 cal BP and 10,730–11,877 cal BP, respectively (Orchiston & Glenie 1978) (Figure 13).

The archaeology of Palana was revisited by Robin Sim in 1989, who obtained a radiocarbon age on charcoal from a culturally sterile level of a relict dune overlying a palaeosol with archaeological deposits. Sim also obtained an age on charcoal collected from a deflated deposit at the foot of the dune face. They gave ages of 4,052 ± 90 BP (ANU-7407) and 4,090 ± 150 BP (ANU-7399), respectively. All of the archaeological evidence at Palana came from a single, thin horizon at deeper and older levels, indicating that the cultural horizon must be older than the calibrated ages of 4,240–4,823 cal BP and 4,089–4,957 cal BP for these stratigraphically higher, and deflated, charcoal samples. A *Cellana solida* shell sample from the archaeological palaeosol deposit at the foot of the dune confirmed the age of this older cultural horizon, giving a direct age of 5,180 ± 70 BP (ANU-7400), calibrating to 5,241–5,785 cal BP (Sim 1991: 82–89).

At the Old Mans Head South midden, near Killiecrankie Beach 7 km south-west of Palana, stone artefacts and shell scatters were also found in deflated sediments on a low limestone ridge (e.g. Orchiston 1979, 1984; Orchiston & Glenie 1978; Sim 1991). Here a *Cellana solida* shell from a cultural shell deposit gave an age of 5,520 ± 80 BP (ANU-7405), calibrating to 5,593–6,161 cal BP (Sim 1991: 101–104). Eleven kilometres to the south-west, towards the north-western corner of Flinders Island, is the Boat Harbour South midden site. Here concentrations of stone artefacts and shell from food refuse have accumulated in patches of deflated sand. A *Cellana solida* shell from one of these cultural deposits gave a radiocarbon age of 6,700 ± 90 BP (ANU-7406), calibrating to 6,858–7,424 cal BP (Sim 1991: 96–101). Three kilometres further to the south-east, near West End Beach, is a small sandy bay. Here, a 6-m-high cliff-face has become exposed through erosion of the dune. Archaeological shell and stone artefacts on a palaeosol are visible in the exposed dune face as well as in the deflated deposits at its foot: the West End midden site. A charcoal sample from the cultural level revealed an age of 6,770 ± 80 BP (ANU-7401), and a *Cellana solida* shell sample also from the cultural level gave an age of 6,370 ± 80 BP (ANU-7402). They calibrate to 7,430–7,721 cal BP and 6,497–7,106 cal BP, respectively (Sim 1991: 89–93).

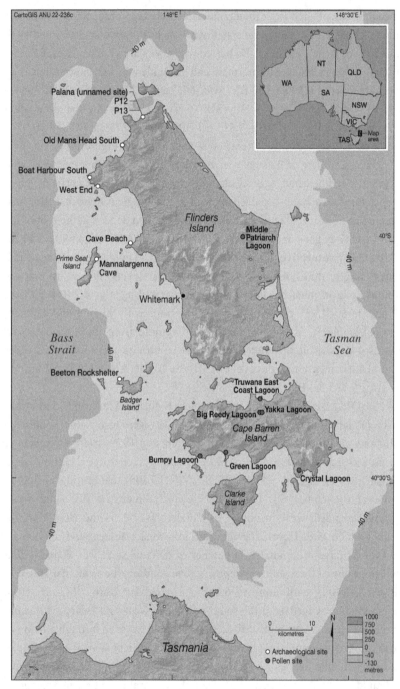

Figure 13 The Furneaux Group, showing the location of all archaeological and pollen sites from which radiocarbon ages have been obtained (artwork by CartoGIS Services, College of Asia and the Pacific, Australian National University).

And midway along the length of Flinders Island, on the western coastline towards the southern end of Marshall Bay 15 km south-east of the West End midden site, is Cave Beach. Here a dune face has been exposed through erosion, again exposing a palaeosol incorporating archaeological shell, along with deflated deposits at the foot of the dune (e.g. Orchiston 1979, 1984). A radiocarbon age of 6,010 ± 90 BP (ANU-7404) on a *Cellana solida* shell dates the cultural layer to 6,111–6,704 cal BP (Sim 1991: 93–96) (a younger charcoal age was interpreted as intrusive by Sim 1991: 96).

These radiocarbon ages indicate that the most recent archaeological evidence of people on the Furneaux Islands dates to:

- Badger Island (12 km^2):

  - 9,194–10,083 cal BP at Beeton Rockshelter (with no signs of human occupation in overlying layers dated to 5,465–6,120 cal BP).

- Prime Seal Island (12 km^2):

  - 8,185–9,423 cal BP at Mannalargenna Cave.

- Flinders Island (1,367 km^2):

  - 10,730–11,877 cal BP at Palana site P13.
  - 7,031–7,615 cal BP at Palana site P12.
  - 6,858–7,424 cal BP at the Boat Harbour South midden.
  - 6,497–7,106 cal BP at the West End midden.
  - 6,111–6,704 cal BP at Cave Beach.
  - 5,593–6,161 cal BP at the Old Mans Head South midden.
  - 5,241–5,785 cal BP at Palana (unnamed site) (with no signs of human occupation in overlying layers dated to 4,240–4,823 cal BP).

The pattern is clear: on the very small Badger and Prime Seal Islands, 12 and 6 km, respectively, from Flinders Island, occupation appears to have ceased by c. 9,000 cal BP, whereas on the large Flinders Island it continued until c. 5,500–6,000 cal BP (keeping in mind that only one site has been excavated from each of Badger and Prime Seal Islands). The cessation of occupation of Badger and Prime Seal Islands corresponds well with their separation from Flinders Island by 9,000 cal BP by rising sea levels. The cessation of occupation on Flinders Island c. 5,500–6,000 cal BP signals that the island continued to be inhabited, or regularly visited by canoes from the Tasmanian mainland, for c. 3,000–3,500 years after its sundering from Tasmania by rising sea levels. At that time, Flinders Island was separated from Tasmania by an approximately 50-km-long sea crossing[1]. This time period corresponds to a period of higher sea level during the Mid-Holocene, which on the Bass-Strait-facing coast of Victoria immediately to the north was 1.1–1.5 m above present sea level between c. 4,700 and 6,300 cal BP (Gardner et al. 2009; Haworth et al. 2002; Kennedy et al. 2021), and it likely remained elevated above present by 0.5 m until around 2,300 cal BP, based on raised *Galeolaria caepitosa* (an inter-tidal tube worm) deposits on King Island (Haworth et al. 2002).

How, then, does the history of cultural fires compare with the pattern of human occupation on the islands, and how would we know that these landscape-scale fires were not wildfires generated naturally such as by lightning?

5.3 Landscape Fires in the Furneaux Group: Towards a History of Cultural Burning

Adeleye et al. (2021) addressed these questions by examining the ten high-resolution (1-cm interval) pollen and charcoal cores from the Furneaux Islands. They differentiated two concepts: the amount of burned vegetation, which they term 'biomass burned' or 'BB' for short, and the frequency of fires, their 'recurrence rate of fire episodes' or 'RRFE'. The amount of BB is a centennial-scale time-averaged proxy for primarily climate-driven biomass accumulation and dryness (and thus burnability) of the vegetation (Ali et al. 2012; Higuera et al. 2010; Vachula 2020). Its palaeo-biogeographic signal is captured in sediment (such as lagoon) deposits by the total charcoal influx of an area for a particular period of time (see Section 4). Across Australia, however, the RRFE in landscapes occupied by people is mainly driven by cultural fire regimes. The RRFE is a proxy for the frequency of charcoal peaks in palaeoecological sequences (e.g. Tinner et al. 1998). In the Furneaux Islands palaeoecological records, it can be measured to decadal-scale accuracy.

Adeleye et al. (2021: 6) found high mean charcoal accumulation rates of 2–7 charcoal particles/cm^2/year in the palaeoecological records of the Furneaux Islands between c. 12,000 and 6,000 cal BP, followed by significantly lower average rates during the Mid- and most of the Late Holocene. Then, during the past 1,000 years, the charcoal accumulation rates increased noticeably to 100 particles/cm^2/year.

However, the pattern of charcoal peaks differed, with a high number of significant ($p < 0.05$) peaks between c. 12,000 and 6,000 cal BP, but

---

[1] The question of how close an island had to be to remain accessible from the Tasmanian mainland in the past has been posed by archaeologists for decades, both with notions of sustainable environments and seafaring technologies in mind; see e.g. Bowdler (2015), Jones (1976, 1977) and Sim (1991, 1994, 1998).

considerably fewer afterwards. The lack of temporal correspondence between the total charcoal influx measures (BB) and the influx peak frequencies (RRFE) gave further confidence that the two measures relate to different phenomena, as described at the start of Section 5.3. '[I]n other words', Adeleye et al. (2021: 6) concluded, 'high RRFE is not always associated with high levels of biomass burning'. Rather, the high incidence of RRFE between c. 12,000 and 6,000 cal BP corresponds with the timing of the persistent presence of human occupation on the islands. This contrasts with the lower total charcoal input (BB) prior to c. 9,000 cal BP, a time when decreased precipitation resulted in reduced levels of biomass accumulation.

Summarising the situation for the Furneaux Islands, Adeleye et al. (2021: 11) concluded that, 'In contrast to increasing RRFE on the [Australian] mainland and western Tasmania, RRFE declined further on the FGI [Furneaux Group of islands] in the last ~5,000 years and overlaps with a reduced human population based on archaeological records [now dated to c. 5,500–6,000 cal BP, see above], which suggests reduced land use.' The reduced occupation of the Furneaux Islands after c. 9,000 cal BP, as indicated by the archaeological evidence, and its cessation by c. 5,500–6,000 cal BP during the Mid-Holocene sea-level high-stand precisely at a time when the coastal plain would have been smaller due to the higher sea level, resulted in less frequent cultural fires, further contributing to biomass accumulation and the widespread burning of wildfires from lightning strikes, such as those that have been documented to rage across whole islands over the past 200 years.

Adeleye et al. successfully investigated the deep-time history of landscape fires, differentiating between cultural burns and wildfires by examining the frequency of charcoal peaks, or RRFEs, as distinct from BB, in sediment sequences (for similar applications in tropical north-eastern Australia, see Haberle et al. 2010). These records do not measure fire severity, but rather fire frequency. Recently, a number of other methods have also been devised to investigate the history of cultural fires versus wildfires from sediment sequences. An exciting development that does measure fire severity is the application of micro-FTIR to charcoal samples, to calculate the maximum temperatures reached during pyrolysis (decomposition under high temperatures) to form biochar (carbon-rich materials caused by burning) on different types of plant matter (Maezumi et al. 2021). By analogue matching, the burning temperatures reached in archaeological and palaeoecological charcoal samples can then be extrapolated, with the potential of differentiating between 'cool' cultural burns and 'hot' wildfires, as described in Section 4 (see also Xiao et al. 2016 for a method that uses H:C ratios to calculate the temperatures reached to heat organic materials).

5.4 Further Readings

Adeleye, M. A., Haberle, S. G., O'Connor, S. E., Stevenson, J. & Bowman, D. M. J. S. (2021). Indigenous fire-managed landscapes in Southeast Australia during the Holocene – New insights from the Furneaux Group islands, Bass Strait. *Fire* 4(17). https://doi.org/10.3390/fire4020017.

Haberle, S. G., Rule, S., Roberts, P. et al. (2010). Paleofire in the wet tropics of northeast Queensland, Australia. *PAGES News* 18(2): 78–80. https://doi.org/10.22498/pages.18.2.78.

Haworth, R. J., Baker, R. & Flood, P. G. (2002). Predicted and observed Holocene sea-levels on the Australian coast: What do they indicate about hydro-isostatic models in far-field sites? *Journal of Quaternary Science: Published for the Quaternary Research Association* 17(5–6): 581–591. https://doi.org/10.1002/jqs.718.

Sim, R. (1998). The archaeology of isolation? Prehistoric occupation in the Furneaux group of islands, Bass Strait, Tasmania. Unpublished PhD thesis, Australian National University, Canberra. http://hdl.handle.net/1885/110266.

6 Conclusion: Implications for the Investigation of Past Cultural Burning Practices Globally

In a recent issue of the journal *Environmental Archaeology*, Christopher Carleton and Mark Collard (2020) identified a number of significant gaps in current themes of landscape archaeology. They singled out the need to pay more attention to the epistemology, and we would add ontology, of causality as it relates to the condition of, and changes in, the landscape and human relations with places. They also urge archaeologists to engage more with aspects of people–place relations that are of interest to present-day communities and policymakers, thereby enhancing the relevance of archaeology to present-day concerns. Landscape fires are one such topic of great interest to which archaeologists, in partnership with local communities and palaeoecologists, can significantly contribute knowledge and perspectives (Marlon et al. 2010; for examples from Ireland, Italy, Portugal, Spain and France, see Carroll et al. 2021; Falcucci et al. 2007; Fernandes et al. 2013; Garcia-Gonzalez et al. 1990; Métailié 2006; Snitker et al. 2022).

Quaternary scientists such as archaeologists, palaeoecologists, palaeoclimatologists and a host of other academic researchers, as well as local communities and Indigenous knowledge-holders, land-care groups and government agencies, have long been interested in vegetation and landscape fire histories. Indeed, such landscape histories have been researched for many decades, especially through pollen and charcoal frequency curves (e.g. David et al. 2012). However, it is only recently that the deep-time history of cultural burning has been targeted for research, mainly in Australia (for influential early examples, see Kershaw 1974; Singh & Geissler 1985 versus Wright 1986). The reasons for this are multiple, including a recent heightened concern for workable land management practices in the face of climate change; a greater awareness by the broader community of the value of Indigenous knowledge, Indigenous land management, and Indigenous place-engagement practices; and the emergence of new analytical methods now capable of differentiating between cultural fires and wildfires from sediment records.

As with so many other archaeological and palaeoecological endeavours, the deep-time history of Indigenous practices can now not only be better investigated but also rendered more meaningful in living landscapes that have never been ceded by Traditional Owners. Vegetation changes are commonly interpreted as cultural signals – such as the elm decline of north and north-west Europe c. 5,000–6,000 cal BP, marked by a reduction of *Ulmus* in pollen sequences (e.g. Kearney & Gearey 2024), or the near-contemporaneity of forest clearance during the European Mesolithic–Neolithic transition (see e.g. Brown 1997), or the burning of swidden agricultural plots in various parts of the world (e.g. Roos et al. 2016). Somewhat surprisingly, landscape-scale burning histories have not usually been looked at as histories of landscape management practices, let alone with the kinds of social, cosmological and emotional engagements and affinities expressed by the Martu and Yanyuwa as discussed by Robert Tonkinson, Doug Bird, Rebecca Bliege Bird and John Bradley. Yet the study of cultural fires brings to light long and continuing relations with the land that tell us as much about social, political and cultural histories as about subsistence economies. The motives for cultural burning and the methods used are distinct to each culture, but there also exist some common themes of taking care of one's own landscape and of placemaking by physically and metaphysically marking the land, in the sense of 'signing the land' with fire (*sensu* Bradley 1997). Studies of cultural burning also signal that physical environments don't just transform through climate change or other natural impacts but have long been actively and variably constructed by the people who engaged with them – an important consideration for researchers interested in notions of carrying capacity, predictive modelling, optimal foraging models and the like (e.g. Bliege Bird et al. 2020). These enhanced dimensions of archaeological and palaeoecological research are made possible by a nuanced pairing with Indigenous knowledge that is more than 'traditional ecological knowledge'. The archaeology of cultural burning is an avenue of research that may well show up new facets and magnitudes of landscape construction, maintenance and social engagement across the world, both for recent times and with much deeper timescales at stake. For this to happen, there first needs to be a will, and an interest, in doing the research in all its technical and fine-grained details.

References

Adeleye, M. A., Haberle, S. G., O'Connor, S. E., Stevenson, J. & Bowman, D. M. J. S. (2021). Indigenous fire-managed landscapes in Southeast Australia during the Holocene – New insights from the Furneaux Group Islands, Bass Strait. *Fire* 4(17). https://doi.org/10.3390/fire4020017.

Adlam, C., Almendariz, D., Goode, R. W., Martinez, D. J. & Middleton, B. R. (2022). Keepers of the flame: Supporting the revitalization of Indigenous cultural burning. *Society & Natural Resources* 35(5): 575–590. https://doi .org/10.1080/08941920.2021.2006385.

Aleman, J. C., Blarquez, O., Bentaleb, I. et al. (2013). Tracking land-cover changes with sedimentary charcoal in the Afrotropics. *The Holocene* 23(12): 1853–1862. https://doi.org/10.1177/0959683613508159.

Ali, A. A., Blarquez, O., Girardin, M. P. et al. (2012). Control of the multi-millennial wildfire size in boreal North America by spring climatic conditions. *Proceedings of the National Academy of Sciences of the United States of America* 109(51): 20966–20970. https://doi.org/10.1073/pnas.1203467109.

Anderson, A., Head, J., Sim, R. & West, D. (1996). Radiocarbon dates on shear-water bones from Beeton Shelter, Badger Island, Bass Strait. *Australian Archaeology* 42: 17–19. www.jstor.org/stable/40287259.

Armstrong, C., Miller, J., McAlvay, A. C., Ritchie, P. M. & Lepofsky, D. (2021). Historical Indigenous land-use explains plant functional trait diversity. *Ecology and Society* 26: 6. https://doi.org/10.5751/ES-12322-260206.

Australasian Fire and Emergency Services Authorities Council (2015). *Overview of Prescribed Burning in Australasia – Report for the National Burning Project: Sub-Project 1*. Nunawading: Australasian Fire and Emergency Services Authorities Council Limited, Valiant Press. https://knowledge.aidr.org.au/ media/4893/overview-of-prescribed-burning-in-australasia.pdf.

Baudin, N. T. (1803). *The Journal of Post Captain Nicolas Baudin, Commander-in-Chief of the Corvettes Geographe and Naturaliste, Assigned by Order of the Government to a Voyage of Discovery* (1974 translation). Adelaide: Libraries Board of South Australia.

Bhattarai, H., Saikawa, E., Wan, X. et al. (2019). Levoglucosan as a tracer of biomass burning: Recent progress and perspectives. *Atmospheric Research* 220: 20–33. https://doi.org/10.1016/j.atmosres.2019.01.004.

Bickford, S., Gell, P. & Hancock, G. J. (2008). Wetland and terrestrial vegetation change since European settlement on the Fleurieu Peninsula, South Australia. *The Holocene* 18(3): 425–436. https://doi.org/10.1177/0959683607087932.

Bickford, S. & Mackey, B. (2004). Reconstructing pre-impact vegetation cover in modified landscapes using environmental modelling, historical surveys and remnant vegetation data: A case study in the Fleurieu Peninsula, South Australia. *Journal of Biogeography* 31(5): 787–805. www.jstor.org/stable/ 3554846.

Binskin, M., Bennett, A. & Macintosh, A. (2020). *Background Paper: Cultural Burning Practices in Australia.* Canberra: Royal Commission into National Natural Disaster Arrangements, Commonwealth of Australia. https://natural disaster.royalcommission.gov.au/publications/background-paper-cultural-burning-practices-australia.

Bird, D. W., Bliege Bird, R., Codding, B. F. & Taylor, N. (2016a). A landscape architecture of fire: Cultural emergence and ecological pyrodiversity in Australia's Western Desert. *Current Anthropology* 57, Supplement 13: S65–S79. https://doi.org/10.1086/685763.

Bird, D. W., Bliege Bird, R. & Codding, B. F. (2016b). Pyrodiversity and the anthropocene: The role of fire in the broad spectrum revolution. *Evolutionary Anthropology* 25: 105–116. https://doi.org/10.1002/evan.21482.

Bird, D. W., Bliege Bird, R. & Parker, C. H. (2005). Aboriginal burning regimes and hunting strategies in Australia's Western Desert. *Human Ecology* 33(4): 443–464. https://doi.org/10.1007/s10745-005-5155-0.

Bird, M. I., Brand, M., Diefendorf, A. F. et al. (2019). Identifying the 'savanna' signature in lacustrine sediments in northern Australia. *Quaternary Science Reviews* 203: 233–247. https://doi.org/10.1016/j.quascirev.2018.11.002.

Blarquez, O., Ali, A. A., Girardin, M. P. et al. (2015). Regional paleofire regimes affected by non-uniform climate, vegetation and human drivers. *Scientific Reports* 5: 13356. https://doi.org/10.1038/srep13356.

Bliege Bird, R. & Bird, D. W. (2021). Climate, landscape diversity, and food sovereignty in arid Australia: The firestick farming hypothesis. *American Journal of Human Biology* 33(4): e23527. https://doi.org/10.1002/ajhb.23527.

Bliege Bird, R., Bird, D. W., Codding, B. F., Parker, C. & Jones, J. H. (2008). The 'fire stick farming' hypothesis: Australian Aboriginal foraging strategies, biodiversity and anthropogenic fire mosaics. *Proceedings of the National Academy of Sciences, USA* 105: 14796–14801. https://doi.org/ 10.1073/pnas.0804757105.

Bliege Bird, R., Bird, D. W., Fernandez, L. et al. (2018). Aboriginal burning promotes fine-scale pyrodiversity and native predators in Australia's Western Desert. *Biological Conservation* 219: 110–118. https://doi.org/10.1016/ j.biocon.2018.01.008.

Bliege Bird, R., Codding, B. F. & Bird, D. W. (2016). Economic, social, and ecological contexts of hunting, sharing, and fire in the Western Desert of

Australia. In Codding, B. F. & Kramer, K. (Eds.), *Why Forage?: Hunters and Gatherers in the Twenty-First Century*, pp. 213–230. Albuquerque: University of New Mexico Press.

Bliege Bird, R., Codding, B. F., Kauhanen, P. & Bird, D. W. (2012). Aboriginal hunting buffers climate-driven fire-size variability in Australia's spinifex grasslands. *Proceedings of the National Academy of Sciences, USA* 109: 10287–10292. https://doi.org/10.1073/pnas.1204585109.

Bliege Bird, R., McGuire, C., Bird, D. W. et al. (2020). Fire mosaics and habitat choice in nomadic foragers. *Proceedings of the National Academy of Sciences of the United States of America* 117(23): 12904–12914. https://doi.org/10.1073/pnas.1921709117.

Bliege Bird, R., Taylor, N., Codding, B. F. & Bird, D. W. (2013). Niche construction and dreaming logic: Aboriginal patch mosaic burning and varanid lizards (*Varanus gouldii*) in Australia. *Proceedings of the Royal Society B* 280: 20132297. https://doi.org/10.1098/rspb.2013.2297.

Bonyhady, T. (2000). *The Colonial Earth*. Carlton: The Miegunyah Press, Melbourne University.

Bowdler, S. (2015). The Bass Strait Islands revisited. *Quaternary International* 385: 206–218. https://doi.org/10.1016/j.quaint.2014.07.047.

Bradley, J. J. (1995). Fire: Emotion and politics – A Yanyuwa case study. In Rose, D. B. (Ed.), *Country in Flames: Proceedings of the 1994 Symposium on Biodiversity and Fire in North Australia*, pp. 25–31. Darwin: North Australia Research Unit, Australian National University.

Bradley, J. J. (1997). *Li-anthawittiyarra*, people of the sea: Yanyuwa relations with their maritime environment. Unpublished PhD thesis, Northern Territory University, Darwin.

Bradley, J. J. & Kearney, A. (2009). Manankurra: What's in a name? Placenames and emotional geographies. In Koch, H. & Hercus, L. (Eds.), *Aboriginal Placenames: Naming and Re-naming the Australian Landscape*, pp. 463–480. Canberra: ANU E Press. https://press-files.anu.edu.au/down loads/press/p17331/pdf/ch182.pdf.

Bradley, J. & Yanyuwa families (2022). *It's Coming from the Times in Front of Us: Country, Kin and the Dugong Hunter Songline*. North Melbourne: Australian Scholarly.

Bradley, R. (1997). *Rock Art and the Prehistory of Atlantic Europe: Signing the Land*. London: Routledge.

Bright, A. & Marranunggu, M. M. (1995). Burn grass. In Rose, D. B. (Ed.), *Country in Flames: Proceedings of the 1994 Symposium on Biodiversity and Fire in North Australia*, pp. 59–62. Darwin: North Australia Research Unit, Australian National University.

Brown, S. (1993). Mannalargenna cave: A Pleistocene site in bass strait. In Smith, M.A., Spriggs, M. & Fankhauser, B. (Eds.), *Sahul in Review: Pleistocene Archaeology in Australia, New Guinea and Island Melanesia.* Occasional Papers in Prehistory 24, pp. 258–271. Canberra: Department of Prehistory, Research School of Pacific Studies, Australian National University.

Brown, T. (1997). Clearances and clearings: Deforestation in Mesolithic/ Neolithic Britain. *Oxford Journal of Archaeology* 16(2): 133–146. https:// doi.org/10.1111/1468-0092.00030.

Buettel, J., David, B., Mullett, R. et al. (Eds.) (2023). *Fires in GunaiKurnai Country: Landscape Fires and Their Impacts on Aboriginal Cultural Heritage Places and Artefacts in Southeastern Australia.* Oxford: Archaeopress. https:// doi.org/10.32028/9781803274812.

Bunting, M. J., Farrell, M., Bayliss, A., Marshall, P. & Whittle, A. (2018). Maps from mud – Using the multiple scenario approach to reconstruct land cover dynamics from pollen records: A case study of two Neolithic landscapes. *Frontiers in Ecology and Evolution* 6: 36. https://doi.org/10.3389/ fevo.2018.00036.

Burch, J., Clark, I. D. & Cahir, F. (2020). Parish plans as a source of evidence of Aboriginal land use in the Mallee back country. *Provenance*: *The Journal of Public Record Office Victoria* 18: 9–21. https://prov.vic.gov.au/explore-col lection/provenance-journal/provenance-2020/parish-plans-source-evidence-aboriginal-land.

Cane, S. (2021). Social and cultural adaptation in the Australian Western Desert. *Journal of the Anthropological Society of South Australia* 45: 74–117.

Carleton, W. C. & Collard, M. (2020). Recent major themes and research areas in the study of human-environment interaction in prehistory. *Environmental Archaeology* 25(1): 114–130. https://doi.org/10.1080/14614103.2018.1560932.

Carroll, M. S., Edgeley, C. M. & Nugent, C. (2021). Traditional use of field burning in Ireland: History, culture and contemporary practice in the uplands. *International Journal of Wildland Fire* 30: 399–409. https://doi.org/10.1071/ WF20127.

Clark, C. (2020). Causes of big bushfires in Australia: High temperatures and rainfall or more fuel? *Journal of Geoscience and Environmental Protection* 8(8): 79–94. www.scirp.org/journal/paperinformation.aspx?paperid=102587.

Clark, R. L. (1983). Pollen and charcoal evidence for the effects of Aboriginal burning on the vegetation of Australia. *Archaeology in Oceania* 18: 32–37.

Constantine, M. & Mooney, S. (2021). Widely used charcoal analysis method in paleo studies involving NaOCl results in loss of charcoal formed below 400 °C. *The Holocene* 32: 1358–1362. https://doi.org/10.1177/09596836211041740.

Constantine, M., Mooney, S., Hibbert, B. et al. (2021). Using charcoal, ATR FTIR and chemometrics to model the intensity of pyrolysis: Exploratory steps towards characterising fire events. *Science of the Total Environment* 783: 147052. https://doi.org/10.1016/j.scitotenv.2021.147052.

David, B., Haberle, S. G. & Walker, D. (2012). Peopled landscapes: The impact of Peter Kershaw on Australian Quaternary science. In David, B. & Haberle, S. G. (Eds.), *Peopled Landscapes: Archaeological and Biogeographic Approaches to Landscapes*, pp. 1–23. Terra Australis 34. Canberra: ANU Press. https://press-files.anu.edu.au/downloads/press/p165471/pdf/ch011.pdf.

Elias, V. O., Simoneit, B. R. T., Cordeiro, R. C. & Turcq, B. (2001). Evaluating levoglucosan as an indicator of biomass burning in Carajás, amazônia: A comparison to the charcoal record. *Geochimica et Cosmochimica Acta* 65(2): 267–272. https://doi.org/10.1016/S0016-7037(00)00522-6.

Falcucci, A., Maiorano, L. & Boitani, L. (2007). Changes in land-use/landcover patterns in Italy and their implications for biodiversity conservation. *Landscape Ecology* 22: 617–631. https://doi.org/10.1007/s10980-006-9056-4.

Federation of Victorian Traditional Owner Corporations (no date). *The Victorian Traditional Owner Cultural Fire Strategy.* https://gunaikurnai.org/wp-content/uploads/2021/07/Victorian-Traditional-Owner-Cultural-Fire-Strategy-ONLINE.pdf.

Fernandes, P. M., Davies, G. M., Ascoli, D. et al. (2013). Prescribed burning in southern Europe: Developing fire management in a dynamic landscape. *Frontiers in Ecology and the Environment* 11: e4–e14. https://doi.org/10.1890/120298.

Finsinger W. & Bonnici, I. (2022). *Tapas: An R Package to Perform Trend and Peaks Analysis.* Zenodo. https://doi.org/10.5281/zenodo.6344463.

Fletcher, M.-S., Romano, A., Connor, S., Mariani, M. & Maezumi, Y. (2021a). Catastrophic bushfires, Indigenous fire knowledge and reframing science in Southeast Australia. *Fire* 4: 61. https://doi.org/10.3390/fire4030061.

Fletcher, M.-S., Hall, T., & Alexandra, A. (2021b). The loss of an Indigenous constructed landscape following British invasion of Australia: An insight into the deep human imprint on the Australian landscape. *Ambio* 50: 138–149. https://doi.org/10.1007/s13280-020-01339-3.

Flinders, M. (1801). *Observations on the Coasts of Van Diemen's Land, on Bass's Strait and Its Islands and on Part of the Coasts of New South Wales: Intended to Accompany the Charts of the Late Discoveries in Those Countries.* London: John Nichols. https://nla.gov.au/nla.obj-125749919/view?partId=nla.obj-156159987#page/n5/mode/1up.

Flinders, M. (1814). *A Voyage to Terra Australis* (1989 facsimile). Adelaide: South Australian Government Printer.

Gammage, B. (2011). *The Biggest Estate on Earth: How Aborigines Made Australia*. Melbourne: Allen & Unwin.

Gammage, B. & Pascoe, B. (2021). *Future Fire, Future Farming*. Port Melbourne: Thames & Hudson.

Garcia-Gonzalez, R., Hidalgo, R. & Montserrrat, C. (1990). Patterns of livestock use in time and space in the summer ranges of the western Pyrenees: A case study in the Aragon Valley. *Mountain Research and Development* 10: 241–255. https://doi.org/10.2307/3673604.

Garde, M., Nadjamerrek, B. L., Kolkkiwarra, M. et al. (2009). The language of fire: Seasonality, resources and landscape burning on the Arnhem Land Plateau. In Russell-Smith, J., Whitehead, P.J. & Cooke, P. M. (Eds.), *Culture, Ecology and Economy of Fire Management in North Australian Savannas: Rekindling the Wurrk Tradition*, pp. 85–164. Melbourne: CSIRO. www.publish.csiro.au/pid/6056.htm.

Gardner, T., Webb, J., Pezzia, C. et al. (2009). Episodic intraplate deformation of stable continental margins: Evidence from Late Neogene and Quaternary marine terraces, Cape Liptrap, Southeastern Australia. *Quaternary Science Reviews* 28(1–2): 39–53. https://doi.org/10.1016/j.quascirev.2008.10.004.

Gaynor, A. & Mclean, I. (2008). Landscape histories: Mapping environmental and ecological change through the landscape art of the Swan River region of western Australia. *Environment and History* 14(2): 187–204.

Gosling, W. D., Cornelissen, H. L. & McMichael, C. N. H. (2019). Reconstructing past fire temperatures from ancient charcoal material. *Palaeogeography, Palaeoclimatology, Palaeoecology* 520: 128–137. https://doi.org/10.1016/j.palaeo.2019.01.029.

Green, P. (1995). Fire in the Kimberley. In Rose, D. B. (Ed.), *Country in Flames: Proceedings of the 1994 Symposium on Biodiversity and Fire in North Australia*, p. 63. Darwin: North Australia Research Unit, Australian National University.

Guérard, E. von (1870). Reply on the critic of Eugène von Guérard's painting of the North Grampians. James Smith Papers MS 212/4, Mitchell Library, State Library of New South Wales, Sydney.

Haberle, S. G., Rule, S., Roberts, P. et al. (2010). Paleofire in the wet tropics of northeast Queensland, Australia. *PAGES News* 18(2): 78–80. https://doi.org/10.22498/pages.18.2.78.

Häggi, C., Hopmans, E. C., Schefuß, E. et al. (2021). Negligible quantities of particulate low-temperature pyrogenic carbon reach the Atlantic Ocean via the Amazon River. *Global Biogeochemical Cycles* 35(9): e2021GB006990. https://doi.org/10.1029/2021GB006990.

Hateley, R. (2010). *The Victorian Bush: Its Original and Natural Condition.* Melbourne: Polybractea Press.

Haworth, R. J., Baker, R. & Flood, P. G. (2002). Predicted and observed Holocene sea-levels on the Australian coast: What do they indicate about hydro-isostatic models in far-field sites? *Journal of Quaternary Science: Published for the Quaternary Research Association* 17(5–6): 581–591. https://doi.org/10.1002/jqs.718.

Head, L. (1989). Prehistoric Aboriginal impacts on Australian vegetation: An assessment of the evidence. *Australian Geographer* 20: 37–46.

Higgins, I. (2020). Indigenous fire practices have been used to quell bushfires for thousands of years, experts say. *ABC News*. www.abc.net.au/news/2020-01-09/indigenous-cultural-fire-burning-method-has-benefits-experts-say/11853096.

Higham, T., Anderson, A., Bronk Ramsey, C. & Tompkins, C. (2005). Diet-derived variations in radiocarbon and stable isotopes: A case study from Shag River Mouth, New Zealand. *Radiocarbon* 47(3): 367–375. https://doi.org/10.1017/S0033822200035141.

Higuera, P. E., Brubaker, L. B., Anderson, P. M., Hu, F. S. & Brown, T.A. (2009). Vegetation mediated the impacts of postglacial climatic change on fire regimes in the south-central Brooks Range, Alaska. *Ecological Monographs* 79: 201–219.

Higuera, P. E., Gavin, D. G., Bartlein, P. J. & Hallett, D. J. (2010). Peak detection in sediment–charcoal records: Impacts of alternative data analysis methods on fire-history interpretations. *International Journal of Wildland Fire* 19(8): 996–1014. https://doi.org/10.1071/WF09134.

Hoffman, K. M., Christanson, A. C., Dickson-Hoyle, S. et al. (2022). The right to burn: Barriers and opportunities for Indigenous-led fire stewardship in Canada. *FACETS* 7: 464–481. https://doi.org/10.1139/facets-2021-0062.

Holmes, M. C. C. & Jampijinpa, W. (2013). Law for country: The structure of Warlpiri ecological knowledge and its application to natural resource management and ecosystem stewardship. *Ecology and Society* 18(3). http://dx.doi.org/10.5751/ES-05537-180319.

Hua, Q., Ulm, S., Yu, K. et al. (2020). Temporal variability in the Holocene marine radiocarbon reservoir effect for the Tropical and South Pacific. *Quaternary Science Reviews* 249: 106613. https://doi.org/10.1016/j.quascirev.2020.106613.

Huffman, M. R. (2013). The many elements of traditional fire knowledge: Synthesis, classification, and aids to cross-cultural problem solving in fire-dependent systems around the world. *Ecology and Society* 18(4). http://dx.doi.org/10.5751/ES-05843-180403.

Huffman, T. N. (2009). A cultural proxy for drought: Ritual burning in the Iron Age of southern Africa. *Journal of Archaeological Science* 36(4): 991–1005. https://doi:10.1016/j.jas.2008.11.026.

Humboldt, A. von. (1849–1858). *Cosmos: A Sketch of a Physical Description of the Universe*. Translated by E. C. Otté. London: Henry G. Bohn.

Ingold, T. (2000). *The Perception of the Environment: Essays on Livelihood, Dwelling and Skill*. London: Routledge.

Jones, R. (1969). Fire-stick farming. *Australian Natural History* 16(7): 224–228.

Jones, R. (1976). Tasmanian aquatic machines and off-shore islands. In Sieveking, G. de G., Longworth, I. H. & Wilson, K. E. (Eds.), *Problems in Economic and Social Archaeology*, pp. 235–263. London: Duckworth.

Jones, R. (1977). Man as an element of a continental fauna: The case of the sundering of the Bassian bridge. In Allen, J., Golson, J. & Jones, R. (Eds.), *Sunda and Sahul: Prehistoric Studies in Southeast Asia, Melanesia and Australia*, pp. 317–386. London: Academic Press.

Jupp, T., Fitzsimons, J., Carr, B. & See, P. (2015). New partnerships for managing large desert landscapes: Experiences from the *Martu Living Deserts Project*. *The Rangeland Journal* 37: 571–582. http://dx.doi.org/10.1071/RJ15047.

Kearney, K. & Gearey, B. R. (2024). The elm decline is dead! Long live declines in elm: Revisiting the chronology of the elm decline in Ireland and its association with the Mesolithic/Neolithic transition. *Environmental Archaeology* 29: 6–19. https://doi.org/10.1080/14614103.2020.1721694.

Kennedy, D. M., Wong, V. N. L. & Jacobsen, G. E. (2021). Holocene infill of the Anglesea Estuary, Victoria: A keep-up estuary in a geologically constrained environment. *Australian Journal of Earth Sciences* 68(6): 839–851. https://doi.org/10.1080/08120099.2021.1879266.

Kershaw, A. P. (1974). A long continuous pollen sequence from northeastern Australia. *Nature* 251: 222–223. https://doi.org/10.1038/251222a0.

Knight, C. A., Anderson, L., Bunting, M. J. et al. (2022). Land management explains major trends in forest structure and composition over the last millennium in California's Klamath Mountains. *Proceedings of the National Academy of Sciences* 119: e2116264119. https://doi.org/10.1073/pnas.2116264119.

Kusmer, A. (2020). California and Australia look to Indigenous land management for fire help. *The World* 1 September. https://theworld.org/stories/2020-09-01/california-and-australia-look-indigenous-land-management-fire-help.

Lambeck, K. & Chappell, J. (2001). Sea level change through the last glacial cycle. *Science* 292: 679–686. www.science.org/doi/10.1126/science.1059549.

Larson E. R., Kipfmueller, K. F. & Johnson, L. B. (2020). People, fire, and pine: Linking human agency and landscape in the boundary waters canoe area wilderness and beyond. *Annals of the American Association of Geographers* 111: 1–25. http://doi.org/10.1080/24694452.2020.1768042.

Latz, P. (1995). Fire in the desert: Increasing biodiversity in the short term, decreasing it in the long term. In Rose, D. B. (Ed.), *Country in Flames: Proceedings of the 1994 Symposium on Biodiversity and Fire in North Australia*, pp. 77–86. Darwin: North Australia Research Unit, Australian National University.

Lewis, H. (1986). Fire technology and resource management in Aboriginal North America and Australia. In Williams, N. & Hunn, E. (Eds.), *Resource Managers: North American and Australian Hunter-Gatherers*, pp. 45–67. Canberra: Australian Institute of Aboriginal Studies.

Lewis, S. E., Sloss, C. R., Murray-Wallace, C. V., Woodroffe, C. D. & Smithers, S. G. (2013). Post-glacial sea-level changes around the Australian margin: A review. *Quaternary Science Reviews* 74: 115–138. https://doi.org/10.1016/j.quascirev.2012.09.006.

Long, J. W., Lake, F. K. & Goode, R. W. (2021). The importance of Indigenous cultural burning in forested regions of the Pacific West, USA. *Forest Ecology and Management* 500: 119597. https://doi.org/10.1016/j.foreco.2021.119597.

Lopes dos Santos, R., De Deckker, P., Hopmans, E. et al. (2013). Abrupt vegetation change after the Late Quaternary megafaunal extinction in south-eastern Australia. *Nature Geoscience* 6: 627–631. https://doi.org/10.1038/ngeo1856.

Lullfitz, A., Dortch, J., Hopper, S. D. et al. (2017). Human niche construction: Noongar evidence in pre-colonial southwestern Australia. *Conservation & Society* 15(2): 201–216. www.environmentandsociety.org/mml/human-niche-construction-noongar-evidence-pre-colonial-southwestern-australia.

Maezumi, S. Y., Elliott, S., Robinson, M. et al. (2022). Legacies of Indigenous land use and cultural burning in the Bolivian Amazon rainforest ecotone. *Philosophical Transactions of the Royal Society B* 377: 20200499. https://doi.org/10.1098/rstb.2020.0499.

Maezumi, S. Y., Gosling, W. D., Kirschner, J. et al. (2021). A modern analogue matching approach to characterize fire temperatures and plant species from charcoal. *Palaeogeography, Palaeoclimatology, Palaeoecology* 578: 110580. https://doi.org/10.1016/j.palaeo.2021.110580.

Mariani, M., Connor, S. E., Fletcher, M.-S. et al. (2017). How old is the Tasmanian cultural landscape? A test of landscape openness using quantitative land-cover reconstructions. *Journal of Biogeography* 44: 2410–2420. http://dx.doi.org/10.1111/jbi.13040.

Mariani, M., Connor, S., Theuerkauf, M. et al. (2022). Disruption of cultural burning promotes shrub encroachment and unprecedented wildfires. *Frontiers in Ecology and the Environment* 20: 292–300. https://doi.org/10.1002/fee.2395.

Marlon, J. R., Bartlein, P. J., Daniau, A. et al. (2013). Global biomass burning: A synthesis and review of Holocene paleofire records and their controls. *Quaternary Science Reviews* 65: 5–25.

Marlon, J. R., Cui, Q., Gaillard, M.-J., McWethy, D. & Walsh, M. (2010). Humans and fire: Consequences of anthropogenic burning during the past 2ka. *PAGES News* 18(2): 80–82. https://doi.org/10.22498/pages.18.2.80.

McMichael, C., Heijink, B., Bush, M. & Gosling, W. (2021). On the scaling and standardization of charcoal data in paleofire reconstructions. *Frontiers of Biogeography* 13(1): e49431. http://doi.org/10.21425/F5FBG49431.

McParland, L. C., Collinson, M. E., Scott, A. C. & Campbell, G. (2009). The use of reflectance values for the interpretation of natural and anthropogenic charcoal assemblages. *Archaeological and Anthropological Sciences* 1: 249. https://doi.org/10.1007/s12520-009-0018-z.

Métailié, J. (2006). Mountain landscape, pastoral management and traditional practices in the Northern Pyrenees (France). In Agnoletti, M. (Ed.), *The Conservation of Cultural Landscapes*, pp. 108–124. Wallingford: CAB International.

Mustaphi, C. J. C. & Pisaric, M. F. J. (2014). A classification for macroscopic charcoal morphologies found in Holocene lacustrine sediments. *Progress in Physical Geography: Earth and Environment* 38(6): 734–754. https://doi.org/10.1177/0309133314548886.

Orchiston, D. W. (1979). Prehistoric man in the Bass Strait region. *See Australia* 2: 130–135.

Orchiston, D. W. (1984). Quaternary environmental changes and Aboriginal man in Bass Strait, Australia. *Man and Environment* 8: 49–60.

Orchiston, D. W. & Glenie, R. C. (1978). Residual Holocene populations in Bassiania: Aboriginal man at Palana, northern Flinders Island. *Australian Archaeology* 8: 127–141. www.jstor.org/stable/40286302.

Pausas, J. & Fernández-Muñoz, S. (2012). Fire regime changes in the Western Mediterranean Basin: From fuel-limited to drought-driven fire regime. *Climatic Change* 110: 215–226. http://doi.org/10.1007/s10584-011-0060-6.

Power, M.J., Marlon, J., Ortiz, N. et al. (2008). Changes in fire regimes since the last glacial maximum: An assessment based on a global synthesis and analysis of charcoal data. *Climate Dynamics* 30: 887–907. http://dx.doi.org/10.1007/s00382-007-0334-x.

Pullin, R. (2009). The Vulkaneifel and Victoria's Western District: Eugene von Guérard and the geognostic landscape. In Marshall, D. R. (Ed.), *Europe and

Australia: Melbourne Art Journal 11–12, pp. 6–33. Melbourne: The Fine Arts Network.

Pullin, R. (2011). *Eugene von Guérard: Nature Revealed*. Melbourne: National Gallery of Victoria.

Pullin, R. (2023). Eugene von Guérard on GunaiKurnai Country 1860–1861: Reading the story of fire in his depictions of the landscape. In Buettel, J., David, B., Mullett, R. et al. (Eds.), *Fires in GunaiKurnai Country: Landscape Fires and Their Impacts on Aboriginal Cultural Heritage Places and Artefacts in Southeastern Australia*, pp. 36–52. Oxford: Archaeopress.

Rehn, E., Rowe, C., Ulm, S. et al.e(2022). Integrating charcoal morphology and stable carbon isotope analysis to identify non-grass elongate charcoal in tropical savannas. *Vegetation History and Archaeobotany* 31: 37–48. https://doi.org/10.1007/s00334-021-00836-z.

Robinson, C., Costello, O., Lockwood, M., Pert, P. & Garnett, S. (2021). *Empowering Indigenous Leadership in Bushfire Recovery, Cultural Burning and Land Management*. Brisbane: NESP Threatened Species Recovery Hub Project 8.2.1 Technical report.

Romano, A. & Fletcher, M.-S. (2019). Evidence for reduced environmental variability in response to increasing human population growth during the late Holocene in northwest Tasmania, Australia. *Quaternary Science Reviews* 97: 193–208. https://doi.org/10.1016/j.quascirev.2018.07.001.

Roos, C. I., Field, J. S. & Dudgeon, J. V. (2016). Anthropogenic burning, agricultural intensification, and landscape transformation in Post-Lapita Fiji. *Journal of Ethnobiology* 36(3): 535–553. https://doi.org/10.2993/0278-0771-36.3.535.

Rose, D. B. (Ed.) (1995). *Country in Flames: Proceedings of the 1994 Symposium on Biodiversity and Fire in North Australia*. Darwin: North Australia Research Unit, Australian National University.

Russell-Smith, J., McCaw, L. & Leavesley, A. (2020). Adaptive prescribed burning in Australia for the early 21st Century – Context, status, challenges. *International Journal of Wildland Fire* 29(5): 305–313. https://doi.org/10.1071/WF20027.

Sim, R. (1991). Prehistoric archaeological investigations on King and Flinders Island, Bass Strait, Tasmania. Unpublished MA Thesis, Australian National University, Canberra. http://hdl.handle.net/1885/117002.

Sim, R. (1994). Prehistoric human occupation in the King and Furneaux Island regions, Bass Strait. In Sullivan, M., Brockwell, S. & Webb, A. (Eds.), *Archaeology in the North: Proceedings of the 1993 Australian Archaeological Association Conference*, pp. 358–374. Darwin: NARU, Australian National University.

Sim, R. (1998). The archaeology of isolation? Prehistoric occupation in the Furneaux group of islands, Bass Strait, Tasmania. Unpublished PhD thesis, Australian National University, Canberra. http://hdl.handle.net/1885/110266.

Singh, G. & Geissler, E. A. (1985). Late Cainozoic history of vegetation, fire, lake levels and climate, at Lake George, New South Wales, Australia. *Philosophical Transactions of the Royal Society of London B: Biological Sciences* 311(1151): 379–447. https://doi.org/10.1098/rstb.1985.0156.

Snitker, G., Roos, C. I., Sullivan III, A. P. et al. (2022). A collaborative agenda for archaeology and fire science. *Nature Ecology & Evolution* 6: 835–839. https://doi.org/10.1038/s41559-022-01759-2.

Stanner, W. E. H. (1965). Aboriginal territorial organization: Estate, range, domain and regime. *Oceania* 36(1): 1–26. www.jstor.org/stable/40329507.

Stanner, W. E. H. (2011). *The Dreaming and Other Essays*. Collingwood: Black Inc. Agenda.

Theden-Ringl, F. (2018). Common cores in the high country: The archaeology and environmental history of the Namadgi Ranges. Unpublished PhD thesis, Australian National University, Canberra.

Thomas, J. (2008). Archaeology, landscape, and dwelling. In David, B. & Thomas, J. (Eds.), *Handbook of Landscape Archaeology*, pp. 300–306. Walnut Creek: Left Coast Press.

Tinner, W., Conedera, M., Ammann, B. et al. (1998). Pollen and charcoal in lake sediments compared with historically documented forest fires in southern Switzerland since AD 1920. *The Holocene* 8(1): 31–42. https://doi.org/10.1191/095968398667205430.

Tonkinson, R. (1978). *The Mardudjara Aborigines: Living the Dream in Australia's Desert*. New York: Holt, Rinehart and Winston.

Umbanhowar, C. E. Jr. & McGrath, M. J. (1998). Experimental production and analysis of microscopic charcoal from wood, leaves and grasses. *The Holocene* 8(3): 341–346. https://doi.org/10.1191/095968398666496051.

Vachula, R. S. (2020). A meta-analytical approach to understanding the charcoal source area problem. *Palaeogeography, Palaeoclimatology, Palaeoecology* 562: 110111. https://doi.org/10.1016/j.palaeo.2020.110111.

Varcoe-Cocks, M. (2011). The act of painting. In Pullin, R. (Ed.), *Eugene von Guérard: Nature Revealed*, pp. 28–35. Melbourne: National Gallery of Victoria.

Whitehair, L., Fulé, P. Z., Sánchez Meador, A., Azpeleta Tarancón, A. & Kim, Y.-S. (2018). Fire regime on a cultural landscape: Navajo Nation. *Ecology and Evolution* 8: 9848–9858. http://doi.org/10.1002/ece3.4470.

Whitlock, C. & Larsen, C. (2001). Charcoal as a fire proxy. In Smol, J. P., Birks, H. J. B. & Last, W. M. (Eds.), *Tracking Environmental Change Using*

Lake Sediments, Volume 3: Terrestrial, Algal, and Siliceous Indicators, pp. 75–97. Dordrecht: Kluwer Academic.

Wright, R. (1986). How old is zone F at Lake George? *Archaeology in Oceania* 21(2): 138–139.

Xiao, X., Chen, Z. & Chen, B. (2016). H/C atomic ratio as a smart linkage between pyrolytic temperatures, aromatic clusters and sorption properties of biochars derived from diverse precursory materials. *Scientific Reports* 6: 22644–22644. https://doi.org/10.1038/srep22644.

Yanyuwa families & Bradley, J. (2016). *Wuka nya-nganunga Li-Yanyuwa Li-Anthawirriyarra: Language for Us, the Yanyuwa Saltwater People – A Yanyuwa Encyclopaedia* Volume 1. North Melbourne: Australian Scholarly Publishing Pty.

Yunupingu, J. (1995). Fire in Arnhem Land. In Rose, D. B. (Ed.), *Country in Flames: Proceedings of the 1994 Symposium on Biodiversity and Fire in North Australia*, pp. 65–66. Darwin: North Australia Research Unit, Australian National University.

Zennaro, P., Kehrwald, N., Marlon, J. et al. (2015). Europe on fire three thousand years ago: Arson or climate? *Geophysical Research Letters* 42(12): 5023–5033. https://doi.org/10.1002/2015GL064259.

Acknowledgements

We thank John Bradley, Doug Bird and Rebecca Bliege Bird, each of whom kindly read through individual sections, made invaluable comments that enabled us to refine both our ideas and the details presented in this Element and/or supplied figures. Thank you to David Kennedy for checking and advising on the latest bathymetry and Holocene sea levels in Bass Strait and the Furneaux Islands. We are very grateful also to Hans Barnard and Willeke Wendrich for inviting us to write this Element, and to Beatrice Rehl and Julia Ford at Cambridge University Press.

For institutional support, we thank the Monash Indigenous Studies Centre at Monash University (Australia), the Centre for Ancient Cultures at Monash University (Australia), the Australian Research Council Centre of Excellence for Australian Biodiversity and Heritage (CABAH, CE170100015), the Australian Research Council Indigenous Discovery Project IN210100055, the Laboratoire EDYTEM and CNRS at the Université Savoie-Mont Blanc (France), and Ministère de la Culture (France).

Cambridge Elements ≡

Current Archaeological Tools and Techniques

Hans Barnard

Cotsen Institute of Archaeology

Hans Barnard was associate adjunct professor in the Department of Near Eastern Languages and Cultures as well as associate researcher at the Cotsen Insitute of Archaeology, both at the University of California, Los Angeles. He currently works at the Roman site of Industria in northern Italy and previously participated in archaeological projects in Armenia, Chile, Egypt, Ethiopia, Italy, Iceland, Panama, Peru, Sudan, Syria, Tunisia, and Yemen.

Willeke Wendrich

Politecnico di Torino

Willeke Wendrich is Professor of Cultural Heritage and Digital Humanities at the Politecnico di Torino (Turin, Italy). Until 2023 she was Professor of Egyptian Archaeology and Digital Humanities at the University of California, Los Angeles, and the first holder of the Joan Silsbee Chair in African Cultural Archaeology. Between 2015 and 2023 she was Firector of the Cotsen Institute of Archaeology, with which she remains affiliated. She managed archaeological projects in Egypt, Ethiopia, Italy, and Yemen, and is on the board of the International Association of Egyptologists, Museo Egizio (Turin, Italy), the Institute for Field Research, and the online UCLA Encyclopedia of Egyptology.

About the Series

Cambridge University Press and the Cotsen Institute of Archaeology at UCLA collaborate on this series of Elements, which aims to facilitate deployment of specific techniques by archaeologists in the field and in the laboratory. It provides readers with a basic understanding of selected techniques, followed by clear instructions how to implement them, or how to collect samples to be analyzed by a third party, and how to approach interpretation of the results.

COTSEN INSTITUTE OF
ARCHAEOLOGY AT UCLA

Cambridge Elements ☰

Current Archaeological Tools and Techniques

Elements in the Series

Archaeological Mapping and Planning
Hans Barnard

Mobile Landscapes and Their Enduring Places
Bruno David, Jean-Jacques Delannoy and Jessie Birkett-Rees

Cultural Burning
Bruno David, Michael-Shawn Fletcher, Simon Connor, Virginia Ruth Pullin,
Jessie Birkett-Rees, Jean-Jacques Delannoy, Michela Mariani, Anthony Romano
and S. Yoshi Maezumi

A full series listing is available at: www.cambridge.org/EATT

Printed in the United States
by Baker & Taylor Publisher Services